(This edition is prepared for Jawaharlal Nehru Technological University, Andhra Pradesh)

Learning English

A Communicative Approach

Course Consultant

A Rama Krishna Rao

Orient BlackSwan

Acknowledgements

The publishers acknowledge the guidance and support received from Dr A Rama Krishna Rao, Professor and Head, Department of Humanities and Social Sciences and Chairman, Board of Studies, JNTU and also members of the Board of Studies (English), JNTU for the publication of this book.

ORIENT BLACKSWAN PRIVATE LIMITED

Registered Office
3-6-752 Himayatnagar, Hyderabad 500 029, India
E-mail: centraloffice@orientblackswan.com

Other Offices
Bangalore / Bhopal / Bhubaneshwar / Chennai / Ernakulam / Guwahati
Hyderabad / Jaipur / Kolkata / Lucknow / Mumbai / New Delhi / Patna

Originally Published by Orient Longman Private Limited 2005, 2006
First edition 2005
Reprinted 2006 (twice), 2007 (thrice), 2008 (twice)
Originally Published as *Reaching for the Stars*
This edition published for JNTU.
First Orient Blackswan Impression 2008
Reprinted 2009, 2013, 2014

Cover and book design

ISBN 978 81 250 2897 0

Typeset in Goudy SansMd Bt 11/13.5 pt by
OSDATA
Hyderabad 500 029

Printed at
SS Colour Impressions Pvt Ltd.
Chennai - 600 106

Published by
Orient Blackswan Private Limited
No. 160, Anna Salai
Chennai 600 002
e-mail:chennai@orientblackswan.com

CONTENTS

1. Astronomy 1
2. Information Technology 17
3. Travel and Transport 31
4. Humour 47
5. Health and Medicine 63
6. Environment 77
7. Inspiration 89
8. Human Interest 107
9. Media 120
Tapescripts 130

Astronomy

OUR PICTURE OF THE UNIVERSE

Long, long ago, it was believed that the world is really a flat plate supported on the back of a giant tortoise standing on an infinite tower of tortoises.Most people would find this picture of our universe rather ridiculous, but why do we think we know better? What do we know about the universe, and how do we know it? Where did the universe come from, and where is it going? Did the universe have a beginning, and if so, what happened *before* then? What is the nature of time? Will it ever come to an end? Recent breakthroughs in physics, made possible in part by fantastic new technologies, suggest answers to some of these long-standing questions. Some day these answers may seem as obvious to us as the earth orbiting the sun—or perhaps as ridiculous as a tower of tortoises. Only time (whatever that may be) will tell.

As long ago as 340 BC the Greek philosopher Aristotle, in his book *On the Heavens*, was able to put forward two good arguments for believing that the earth was a round sphere rather than a flat plate. First, he realised that eclipses of the moon were caused by the earth coming between the sun and the moon. The earth's shadow on the moon was always round, which would be true only if the earth was spherical. Second, the Greeks knew from their travels that the North Star appeared lower in the sky when viewed in the south than it did in more northerly regions. (Since the North Star lies over the North Pole, it appears to be directly above an observer at the North Pole, but to someone looking from the equator, it appears to lie just at the horizon.)

Aristotle thought that the earth was stationary and that the sun, the moon, the planets, and the stars moved in circular orbits about the earth. This idea was elaborated by Ptolemy in the second century AD into a complete cosmological model. The earth stood at the centre, surrounded by eight spheres that carried the moon, the sun, the stars, and the five planets known at the time: Mercury, Venus, Mars, Jupiter, and Saturn. The planets themselves moved on smaller circles attached to their respective spheres in order to account for their rather complicated observed paths in the sky. The outermost sphere carried the so-called fixed stars, which always stay in the same positions relative to each other but which rotate together across the sky. What lay beyond the last sphere was never made very clear, but it certainly was not part of mankind's observable universe.

A simpler model, however, was proposed in 1514 by a Polish priest, Nicholas Copernicus. His idea was that the sun was stationary at the centre and that the earth and the planets moved in circular orbits around the sun. Nearly a century passed before this idea was taken seriously. Then two astronomers—the German, Johannes Kepler, and the Italian, Galileo Galilei—started publicly to support the Copernican theory, despite the fact that the orbits it predicted did not quite match the ones observed. The death blow to the Aristotelian–Ptolemaic theory came in 1609. In that year, Galileo started observing the night sky with a telescope, which had just been invented. When he looked at the planet Jupiter, Galileo found that it was accompanied by several small satellites or moons that orbited around it. This implied that everything did *not* have to orbit directly around the earth, as Aristotle and Ptolemy had thought. At the same time, Johannes Kepler had modified Copernicus's theory, suggesting that the planets moved not in circles but in ellipses. The predictions now finally matched the observations, but Kepler could not reconcile them with his idea that the planets were made to orbit the sun by magnetic forces. An explanation was provided only much later, in 1687, when Sir Isaac Newton published his *Philosophiae Naturalis Principia Mathematica*, in which he not only put forward a theory of how bodies move in space and time, but also developed the complicated mathematics needed to analyse those motions. In addition, Newton postulated a law of universal gravitation according to which each body in the universe was attracted toward every other body by a force that was stronger, the more massive the bodies and the closer they were to each other. It was this same force that caused objects to fall to the ground.

Newton went on to show that, according to his law, gravity causes the moon to move in an elliptical orbit around the earth and causes the earth and the planets to follow elliptical paths around the sun.

Newton realised that, according to his theory of gravity, the stars should attract each other, so it seemed they could not remain essentially motionless. Would they not all fall together at some point? He argued that this would indeed happen if there were only a finite number of stars distributed over a finite region of space but reasoned that if, on the other hand, there were an infinite number of stars, distributed more or less uniformly over infinite space, this would not happen, because there would not be any central point for them to fall to.

This argument is an instance of the pitfalls that you can encounter in talking about infinity. In an infinite universe, every point can be regarded as the centre, because every point has an infinite number of stars on each side of it. The correct approach, it was realised only much later, is to consider the finite situation, in which the stars all fall in on each other, and then to ask how things change if one adds more stars roughly uniformly distributed outside this region. According to Newton's law, the extra stars would make no difference at all to the original ones on average, so the stars would fall in just as fast. We can add as many stars as we like, but they will still always collapse in on themselves. We now know it is impossible to have an infinite static model of the universe in which gravity is always attractive.

It is an interesting reflection on the general climate of thought before the twentieth century that no one had suggested that the universe was expanding or contracting. It was generally accepted that either the universe had existed forever in an unchanging state, or that it had been created at a finite time in the past more or less as we observe it today. Even those who realised that Newton's theory of gravity showed that the universe could not be static did not think to suggest that it might be expanding. Instead, they attempted to modify the theory by making the gravitational force repulsive at very large distances. This did not significantly affect their predictions of the motions of the planets, but it allowed an infinite distribution of stars to remain in equilibrium—with the attractive forces between nearby stars balanced by the repulsive forces from those that were farther away. However, we now believe such an equilibrium would be unstable: if the stars in some region got only slightly nearer each other, the attractive forces between them would become stronger and dominate over the repulsive forces so that the stars would continue to fall toward each other. On the other hand, if the stars got a bit farther away from each other, the repulsive forces would dominate and drive them farther apart.

When most people believed in an essentially static and unchanging universe, the question of whether or not it had a beginning was really one of metaphysics or theology. One could account for what was observed equally well on the theory that the universe had existed forever or on the theory that it was set in motion at some finite time in such a manner as to look as though it had existed forever. But in 1929, Edwin Hubble made the landmark observation that wherever you look, distant galaxies are moving rapidly away from us. In other words, the universe is expanding. This means that at earlier times objects would have been closer together. In fact, it seemed that there was a time, about ten or twenty thousand million years ago, when they were all at exactly the same place and when, therefore, the density of the universe was infinite. This discovery finally brought the question of the beginning of the universe into the realm of science.

Hubble's observations suggested that there was a time, called the Big Bang, when the universe was infinitesimally small and infinitely dense. Under such conditions all the laws of science, and therefore all ability to predict the future, would break down. One may say that time had a beginning at the Big Bang, in the sense that earlier times simply would not be defined. It should be emphasised that this beginning in time is very different from those that had been considered previously. In an unchanging universe a beginning in time is something that has to be imposed by some being outside the universe; there is no physical necessity for a beginning. One can imagine that God created the universe at literally any time in the past. On the other hand, if the universe is expanding, there may be physical reasons why there had to be a beginning. One could still imagine that God created the universe at the instant of the

Big Bang, or even afterwards in just such a way as to make it look as though there had been a Big Bang, but it would be meaningless to suppose that it was created before the Big Bang.

In order to talk about the nature of the universe and to discuss questions such as whether it has a beginning or an end, you have to be clear about what a scientific theory is. I shall take the simple-minded view that a theory is just a model of the universe, or a restricted part of it, and a set of rules that relate quantities in the model to observations that we make. It exists only in our minds and does not have any other reality. A theory is a good theory if it satisfies two requirements: it must accurately describe a large class of observations on the basis of a model that contains only a few arbitrary elements, and it must make definite predictions about the results of future observations. For example, Aristotle's theory that everything was made out of four elements, earth, air, fire, and water, was simple enough to qualify, but it did not make any definite predictions. On the other hand, Newton's theory of gravity was based on an even simpler model, in which bodies attracted each other with a force that was proportional to a quantity called their mass and inversely proportional to the square of the distance between them. Yet it predicts the motions of the sun, the moon, and the planets to a high degree of accuracy.

Any physical theory is always provisional, in the sense that it is only a hypothesis. As philosopher of science Karl Popper has emphasised, a good theory is characterised by the fact that it makes a number of predictions that could in principle be disproved or falsified by observation. Each time new experiments are observed to agree with the predictions the theory survives, and our confidence in it is increased; but if ever a new observation is found to disagree, we have to abandon or modify the theory. In practice, what often happens is that a new theory is devised that is really an extension of the previous theory. For example, Einstein's general theory of relativity predicted a slightly different motion from Newton's theory of gravity.

The eventual goal of science is to provide a single theory that describes the whole universe. However, the approach most scientists actually follow is to separate the problem into two parts. First, there are the laws that tell us how the universe changes with time. Second, there is the question of the initial state of the universe. Some people feel that science should be concerned with only the first part; they regard the question of the initial situation as a matter for metaphysics or religion. They would say that God, being omnipotent, could have started the universe off any way he wanted. That may be so, but it appears that he chose to make it evolve in a very regular way according to certain laws. It therefore seems equally reasonable to suppose that there are also laws governing the initial state.

It turns out to be very difficult to devise a theory to describe the universe all in one go. Instead, we break the problem up into bits and invent a number of partial theories. Each of these partial theories describes and predicts a certain limited class of observations, neglecting the effects of

other quantities, or representing them by simple sets of numbers. It may be that this approach is completely wrong. If everything in the universe depends on everything else in a fundamental way, it might be impossible to get close to a full solution by investigating parts of the problem in isolation. Nevertheless, it is certainly the way that we have made progress in the past. The classic example again is the Newtonian theory of gravity, which tells us that the gravitational force between two bodies depends only on one number associated with each body, its mass, but is otherwise independent of what the bodies are made of. Thus one does not need to have a theory of the structure and constitution of the sun and the planets in order to calculate their orbits.

Today scientists describe the universe in terms of two basic partial theories—the general theory of relativity and quantum mechanics, the great intellectual achievements of the first half of this century. The general theory of relativity describes the force of gravity and the large-scale structure of the universe, that is, the structure on scales from only a few miles to as large as a million million million million (1 with twenty-four zeros after it) miles, the size of the observable universe. Quantum mechanics, on the other hand, deals with phenomena on extremely small scales, such as a millionth of a millionth of an inch. Unfortunately, however, these two theories are known to be inconsistent with each other—they cannot both be correct. One of the major endeavours in physics today is the search for a new theory that will incorporate them both—a quantum theory of gravity. We do not yet have such a theory, and we may still be a long way from having, one, but we do already know many of the properties that it must have.

Now, if you believe that the universe is not arbitrary, but is governed by definite laws, you ultimately have to combine the partial theories into a complete unified theory that will describe everything in the universe. Because the partial theories that we already have are sufficient to make accurate predictions in all but the most extreme situations, the search for the ultimate theory of the universe seems difficult to justify on practical grounds. (It is worth noting, though, that similar arguments could have been used against both relativity and quantum mechanics, and these theories have given us both nuclear energy and the microelectronics revolution!) The discovery of a complete unified theory, therefore, may not aid the survival of our species. It may not even affect our lifestyle. But ever since the dawn of civilisation, people have not been content to see events as unconnected and inexplicable. They have craved an understanding of the underlying order in the world. Today we still yearn to know why we are here and where we came from. Humanity's deepest desire for knowledge is justification enough for our continuing quest. And our goal is nothing less than a complete description of the universe we live in.

[Adapted from Stephen Hawking, *A Brief History of Time*]

Comprehension

A. *Read the given text carefully and answer the following questions briefly.*

1. What was Aristotle's basis for believing that the earth was spherical?
2. What were Aristotle's and Copernicus's models of the universe and how was the latter supported by Galileo?
3. What was the gist of Newton's theory of gravity?
4. Why does Stephen Hawking think there is need to develop a complete unified theory of the universe? Has it been done at all?
5. Which human yearning is justification enough for the continued search for this complete unified theory of the universe and why?

B. *Choose from a, b* and *c the correct endings to the following sentences.*

1. Aristotle realised that eclipses of the moon were caused by
   a. the sun coming between the earth and the moon.
   b. the earth coming between the sun and the moon.
   c. the moon coming between the earth and the sun.

2. Galileo's observation of the planet Jupiter indicated that
   a. the earth was at the centre of the universe.
   b. the planets moved around Jupiter.
   c. the earth need not be at the centre of the universe.
3. Newton postulated a law of universal gravitation according to which
   a. each body in the universe was drawn away from another body by strong forces.
   b. each body in the universe moved independent of every other body.
   c. each body in the universe was attracted toward every other body by a strong force.
4. A good theory must accurately describe a class of observations on the basis of a model and
   a. it must be able to make observations based on past theories.
   b. it must make definite predictions about the results of future observations.
   c. it must present good models for further research and study.

Vocabulary

An antonym is a word that is opposite in meaning to another word. The antonym of a word could either be a completely different word as in *happy* and *sad* or a word formed by a prefix as in *direct* and *indirect*.

A. *List the antonyms of the following words that appear in the given text.*

1. perfect	6. believing	11. similar
2. stationary	7. definite	12. accurately
3. partial	8. complicated	13. practical
4. superior	9. expanding	14. general
5. major	10. finite	15. single

B. *Look up the following words in a dictionary. Find out how each word is pronounced, which syllable of the word is stressed, the part of speech it belongs to (noun, verb, pronoun, etc.), and in case the word has more than one core meaning, identify the sense in which the word is used in the text that you have just read.*

1. fantastic	2. tortoise	3. endeavour
4. yearn	5. elliptical	6. principle

A phrasal verb that consists of a verb followed by an adverb or a preposition functions as an independent verb, or as a complete unit of meaning, for example 'ask for' and 'ask after'. You can refer to a dictionary to find out the exact meaning of any phrasal verb that you are not familiar with.

C. *Fill in the blanks in the following sentences with appropriate tense forms of phrasal verbs chosen from those given in the box.*

run across	run away with	run (something) by/past	run on
run up against	run through	run out	

1. Ahmed has................ of subjects to discuss with the man sitting next to him.
2. The children's imagination was .... them, and their story sounded more and more incredible.
3. Could this exercise be .... your language teacher, please.
4. I .... an interesting person today on my way to college.
5. Shall we .... the schedule for the seminar before we leave?
6. These are some of the problems that Sujata .... at the booking office tomorrow.
7. The play .... until very late last night.

Grammar

A. *Punctuate the passages below so that they make sense.*

1. There was once a giant who was too big to be seen as he walked about the space between his legs was so great that nobody could see as far as from one side to the other and his head was so high in the sky that nobody's eyes were strong enough to see the top of him not being able to take him in all at once nobody therefore knew that the giant existed sometimes men felt his footsteps shake the earth and then they said there has been another earthquake and sometimes they felt his shadow pass over them and they said what a dark day it is and sometimes when he stooped to scratch his leg they felt him breathe and said phew what a wind and that was as much as they knew about him.

2. in every country people imagine that they are the best and the cleverest and the others are not as good as they are the englishman thinks that he and his country are the best the frenchman is very proud of france and everything french the germans and the italians think no end of their countries and many indians imagine that india is in many ways the greatest country in the world this is all conceit everybody wants to think well of himself and his country
3. man as a rule longs for peace and happiness he dreads all sorrows misfortunes and calamities such as failures in examinations loss of money deaths in the family and suffering from disease life should be for him a continuous flow of success peace and prosperity but man does not realise that adversity has its own advantages it is during moments of great stress suffering and misfortune that the best faculties in man have shown forth it is during such times that he turns contemplative and philosophical and becomes a believer in divine forces when kunti the mother of the pandava princes was asked by krishna to choose a boon she promptly asked for a life of adversity which alone would fix her mind on god.

B. *The following passage has not been edited. There is one error in each line. Underline each error and write the correct word in the space provided. The first correction has been done as an example.*

Many psychologists see leisure as a essential counterbalance	an
for work. Overwork can contribute to harmful stress and can	(1) ________
reduce an ability to concentrate and to perform a job effectively.	(2) ________
Leisurely activities refresh and revitalise the body and the mind.	(3) ________
The brain needs stimulation of various kind in order to	(4) ________
stay on top form. Some of us do not mind repetitive daily	(5) ________
routines, but others are bored with them, especially if they	(6) ________
continues over weeks and months. When this occurs, the brain	(7) ________
adapts by reducing it's level of activity, but then the brain	(8) ________
has mechanisms that arouse a need for stimulation.	

Listening

A. *Your teacher will play to you numbered words on tape. For each word that you listen to, you will find a set of printed words below. Tick the printed word that corresponds to the spoken word.*

1.	a. piece	b. place	c. praise	d. pace
2.	a. thin	b. tin	c. din	d. teen
3.	a. squeak	b. speak	c. streak	d. sweet
4.	a. mental	b. mantle	c. mentor	d. mended
5.	a. person	b. prism	c. prison	d. present
6.	a. win	b. when	c. wane	d. whine

B. *Your teacher will play to you numbered sentences on tape. For each sentence that you listen to, you will find a set of printed words below. Tick the printed word that corresponds to one in the spoken sentence.*

1.	a. pale	b. fan	c. pain	d. pan
2.	a. trade	b. thread	c. tread	d. threat
3.	a. silver	b. slither	c. liver	d. sliver
4.	a. tome	b. ton	c. tone	d. dome
5.	a. frugal	b. fuel	c. feudal	d. dual
6.	a. seat	b. sheet	c. sleet	d. street

Speaking

Listen to two dialogues that your teacher will play for you on tape and also read their transcripts in your book. Pay attention to the italicised expressions in the transcripts of the dialogues presenting situations where people greet and take leave of one another. Dialogue 1 occurs in a formal situation while dialogue 2 is informal.

Dialogue 1 (formal)

(Mr Anand meets Amita, a student who lives in his neighbourhood, at a bookstore. They have met before, but do not know each other very well.)

Amita: *Good morning,* Mr Anand. *How're you?*

Mr Anand: *Good morning,* Amita. *I'm very well, thank you. What about you?*

Amita: *I'm fine, thanks. We haven't met for quite sometime, have we?*

Mr Anand: Yes, you're right. I have been away in Nagpur. Have you found something interesting to buy?

Amita: No, not really. I just came in a few minutes ago.

Mr Anand: Well, *it was nice meeting you,* Amita. I could have given you a lift home but *I'm afraid I have to rush to keep an appointment. I do hope you'll excuse me.*

Amita: Oh, *that's quite all right,* Mr Anand. *I hope we can meet again soon.*

Mr Anand: *Yes, please do come over sometime. Bye!*

Amita: *Bye, bye,* Mr Anand!

Dialogue 2 (informal)

(Barkha meets Farha, who used to be a classmate at school, after a long time at a wedding.)

Barkha: *Hello,* Farha! *What a lovely surprise! Good to see you after so long.*

Farha: *Hi,* Barkha! *Yes, it's great to see you too! How're you and where have you been?*

Barkha: *Just fine, thanks.* I was away in Aligarh. And *how are things with you?*

Farha: *Everything's okay, thanks.* Hey, *we must meet and catch up on all that's been happening.*

Barkha: *We must do that.* Let me jot down your telephone number.

Farha: Here, I'll write it down for you. *Wish I could have stayed longer, but I must run.* Have to pick up Mother from the station.

Barkha: *Sure, see you sometime. Bye!*

Farha: *Bye, bye!*

Exercise A

You will hear on tape some expressions used to greet people and take leave of them. Listen to each item and repeat it using the pronunciation and intonation that you hear on tape. Note the use of contracted forms such as 'I'm' for 'I am' and 'you'll' for 'you will'.

- Good morning, how are you?
- I'm very well, thank you. What about you?
- I'm fine, thanks.
- We haven't met for quite sometime, have we?
- It's a pleasure to see you.
- It was nice meeting you, but I'm afraid I have to go now.
- I must leave. I hope you'll excuse me.
- That's quite all right. I hope we can meet again soon.
- Yes, we must.
- Yes, I hope so too.
- Yes, please do come over.
- Bye, bye!

Exercise B

You will now hear on tape some expressions used in informal situations to greet people and take leave of them. Listen to each item and repeat it as you did in Exercise A.

- Hello! What a lovely surprise!
- Good to see you after so long.
- Hi! Its great to see you too.
- How're you and where have you been?
- Just fine, thanks. How're things with you?
- Everything's okay, thanks.
- We must meet and catch up on what's happening.
- Yes, we must do that.
- Wish I could have stayed longer, but I must run.
- Sure, see you sometime. Bye, bye!

Exercise C

Working in pairs, write and enact the following situations in the form of brief dialogues choosing appropriate expressions from those given above.

1. Nita is on her way to her violin class. She meets Dr Prakash, her father's boss, outside the music school. The two persons greet each other and exchange a few words before taking leave.
2. Abhay runs into Abdul, a friend, at a supermarket. The two men greet each other and exchange a few words before taking leave.

Writing

Paragraph writing

Some useful points to remember

- Every paragraph should have unity of theme which means that it should be built around a single idea expressed in a topic sentence.
- The topic sentence can be placed at the beginning, somewhere within or at the end of the paragraph, though in texts relating to science and technology, the first position is most often preferred.
- Do not make your paragraphs too long.
- A paragraph must have the feature of coherence, which means that all the sentences in it must be arranged in a way that indicates a logical progression of thought.
- Coherence in a paragraph can be achieved by arranging its sentences according to chronological, spatial or logical order. The first is useful in describing events, the second in describing a scene and the third in describing phenomena where a cause-and-effect relation needs to be presented.
- A second way of writing a coherent paragraph is by using connectives, such as 'therefore', 'however', 'also', 'thus', 'finally', etc.
- A third way of ensuring coherence in a paragraph is by the use of pronouns and other reference words.
- Use variety in sentence length and structure to make your paragraphs more interesting.

Read the specimen paragraph below and note how the main idea in the highlighted topic sentence is developed logically by the sentences that follow.

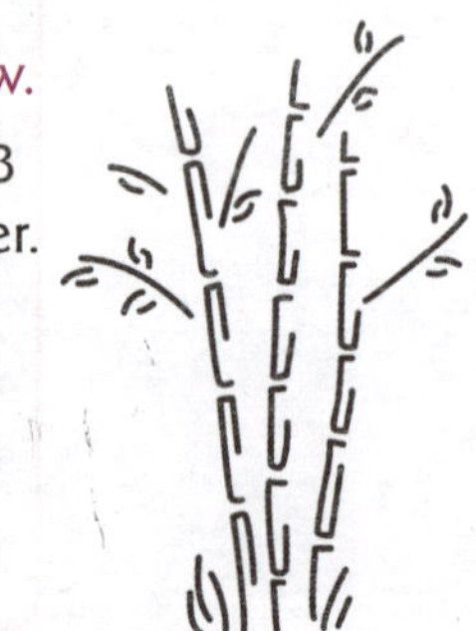

The commercial uses of bamboo are astonishing. India produces over 3 million tonnes of bamboo annually, and nearly half of it is turned into paper. Another important use of bamboo is in housing. Instead of costly timber, bamboo can be used in the construction of houses. In Colombia, bamboo used in house structures is covered with plaster. Bamboo can replace even steel in many of its uses. Concrete reinforced with bamboo is sufficiently strong for most uses. In Assam, suspension bridges have been built using bamboo. Scientists at the Forest Research Institute, Dehra Dun, are working on the extraction of diesel fuel from the jointed stem of bamboo. With its network of rhizomes and roots, bamboo also plays an important role in the prevention of soil erosion.

Exercises

A. *Rearrange each group of jumbled sentences below so as to have well-written paragraphs.*

1. a. Ordinary steel contains 0.06% to 0.12% of carbon.
   b. Stainless steel contains chromium, and the steel used in making permanent magnets contains cobalt.
   c. This small quantity of carbon turns iron, which in its pure state is soft, into hard and elastic steel.
   d. Besides these common varieties of steel, there are others designed by the metallurgist, which possess very special properties and answer very special needs.
   e. By the addition of elements other than carbon, we obtain steel adapted to particular uses in technology.
   f. The term 'steel' refers to a large number of alloys of iron.
2. a. It contains, of course, the meanings of 'difficult words'.
   b. One of the most important reference books that you must possess is a dictionary.
   c. It also gives you the pronunciation of the words.
   d. You do possess one, perhaps, but I doubt whether you are aware of the different kinds of information it contains.
   e. The dictionary can be referred to for the various grammatical forms of the words.
   f. Every college dictionary should provide at least these four kinds of information about words, namely pronunciation, meaning, grammatical patterns and usage.
   g. Finally, a good dictionary contains illustrative sentences or phrases, showing how words are actually used.
3. a. There are direct intellectual effects: the dispelling of many traditional beliefs, and the adoption of others suggested by the success of the scientific method.
   b. Then, chiefly as a consequence of new techniques, there are profound changes in social organisation, which are bringing about corresponding political changes.
   c. The effects of science are of various, very different kinds.
   d. Then there are effects on technique in industry and war.
   e. Finally, as a result of the new control over the environment which scientific knowledge has conferred, a new philosophy is growing up, involving a changed conception of the place of human beings in the universe.
4. a. They are chemistry, physics, physiology or medicine, literature and peace.
   b. It is awarded from funds bequeathed by Alfred Nobel, a Swedish inventor and philanthropist.
   c. In 1969 economics was added to the list.
   d. Nobel's will designated six areas for which prizes could be awarded.

e. Prizes in these seven areas are presented in December every year, in the presence of the King of Sweden, as a fitting tribute to Alfred Nobel.

f. The Nobel Prize is considered one of the most prestigious awards made to people whose work benefits humanity.

g. The funds are administered by the Nobel Foundation in Stockholm.

B. *Write well-constructed paragraphs on any two of the following topics. Use examples, arguments or explanations to amplify the statements. Discuss the topic with a partner before you start writing.*

1. Education can be meaningful only when the syllabus is relevant and when the students enjoy learning.
2. It is important for two people to know and understand each other before they decide to get married.
3. Reasons for promoting the widespread use of solar energy.

Description

Some useful points to remember

- The subject of a description can be people and places, objects or processes and mechanisms.
- To write a good description you should know why it is written and who it is written for.
- Because describing something involves recreating your experiences and impressions, it is important that you perceive accurately the subject of your description before you begin writing.
- Be as specific as you can and give as many details as possible.
- Avoid using general, vague or abstract words in your descriptions.
- In describing processes and mechanisms, remember to use the passive voice and also follow a sequence that can be indicated by words such as 'firstly', 'secondly', 'then', 'next' and 'finally'.

Exercises

A. *Read the two descriptions of a pressure cooker below. The first is a description of its parts and working and the second is a description meant for advertising.*

- A pressure cooker is a vessel in which food is cooked in steam under pressure. It consists of a very strong vessel made of aluminium alloy, with a lid that fits tightly on the top. The lid can be sealed on to the vessel by means of a rubber ring. At the centre of the lid there is a vent, or hole through which steam can escape. The food to be cooked is placed in a smaller vessel inside the cooker and a little water is poured into the outer vessel. Water boils in the vessel, and steam begins to escape through the vent. Then the steam is stopped by placing a weight on the vent. Steam pressure inside increases and the temperature rises. So the food gets cooked at a higher temperature. This takes only one-third of the time taken by the ordinary method.

- The Cookwick pressure cooker has a capacity of 8 litres. The pressure can be varied using two separate weight-valves. A newly designed safety plug makes Cookwick much safer than other makes. Made of aluminium alloy by a very special process, your Cookwick pressure cooker will last a lifetime.

Using the above paragraphs as models, write two descriptions of one of the following objects, the first describing its parts and functions and the second as in an advertisement.

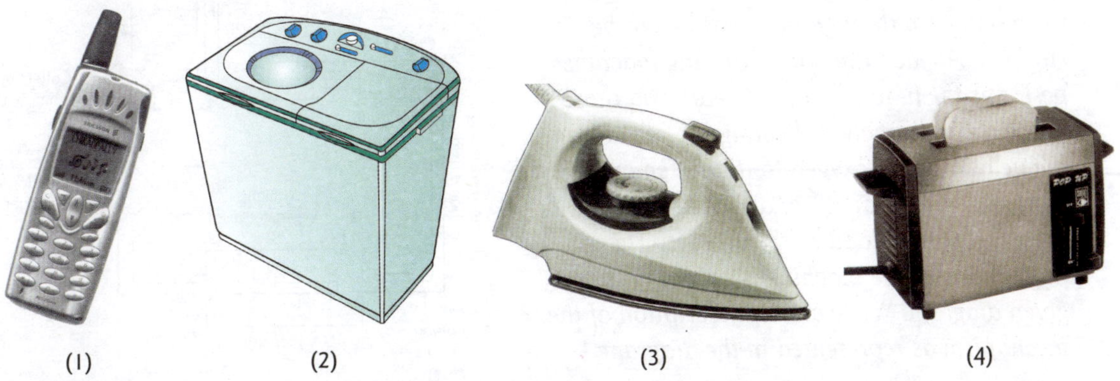

(1) (2) (3) (4)

B. *Write a description of a person you know. Try to include the following information: Is he or she tall or short, fat or thin? What is the shape of the person's face—round, oval, square or triangular? Does the person have thick hair? Is the hair straight or curly? Is the forehead broad or narrow? Is the nose straight or crooked or upturned or flat? Are the lips full or thin? How is he or she dressed? What impression do you get of his or her personality from the person's appearance and dress?*

C. *Visit an ancient monument, a modern factory or a busy marketplace in your village, town or city. Look around carefully and observe the smallest details about its location, size, layout, and the sights and sounds that you find there. Write a description for your friend who is interested in the place.*

D. *Here are three simple processes. Choose any one of them, and in small groups, discuss how the process is carried out. Write two descriptions, one describing the process step by step for a person who wants to learn to do it, and the second reporting the steps taken after the process has been completed.*

1. how to make idlis/chapatis
2. how to administer first aid to a person with a deep, bleeding wound on the foot
3. how to take pictures with a camera

You can refer to the following models before you begin.

beetroot salad

2 or 3 beetroots	salt
2 tsp. salad oil	pepper
¼ cup vinegar	celery

- Boil or bake beetroots until tender. Peel and shred. Sprinkle salt and a dash of pepper. Add oil and vinegar. Add celery.
- The beetroots were boiled until tender. Then they were peeled and shredded. Next, salt and a dash of pepper were sprinkled. Finally, oil, vinegar and celery were added to the salad.

E. *When operations are performed on the heart, the blood flow through the heart has to be stopped. At such times a heart-lung machine performs the functions of the heart and those of the lungs, namely, collecting the blood from the veins, adding oxygen to it and removing carbon dioxide from it, and then supplying the oxygenated blood to the arteries. The functioning of the machine is shown in the given diagram. Write a brief description of the mechanism as represented in the diagram.*

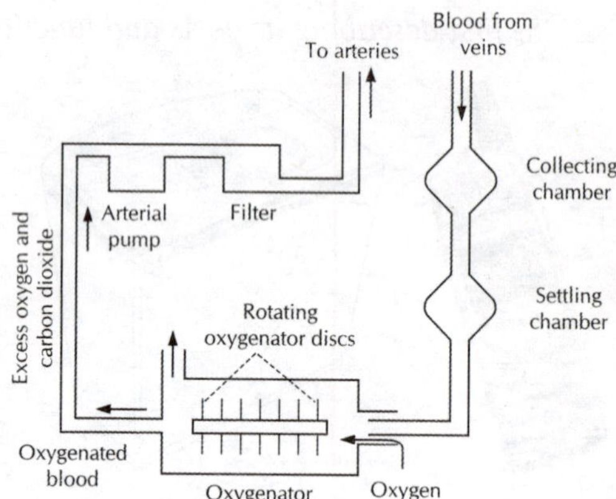

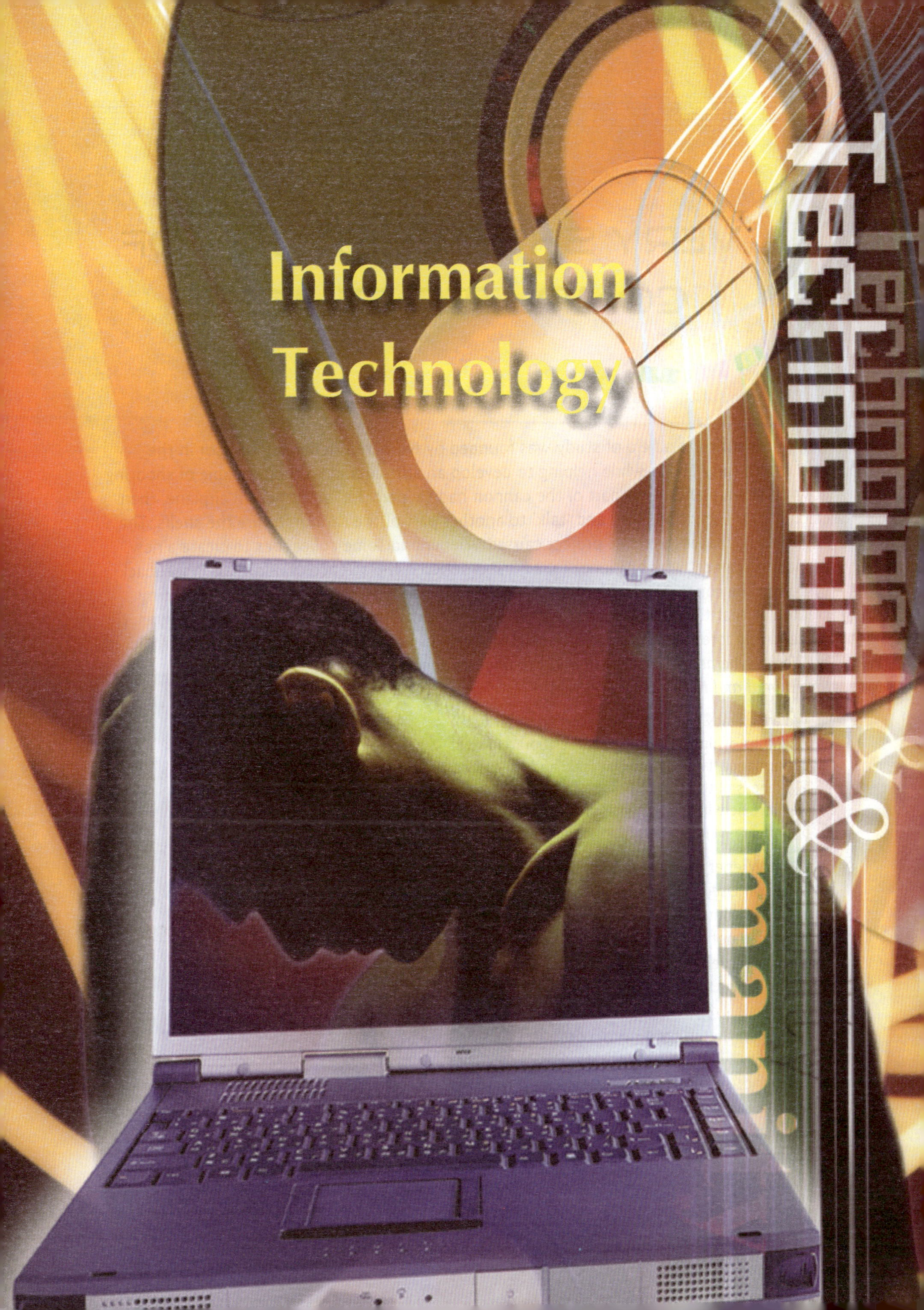
Information
Technology
Technology & Human

A VERY SHORT HISTORY OF COMPUTER ETHICS

Computer ethics as a field of study was founded by Norbert Wiener, a professor in the MIT, in the early 1940s while helping to develop an anti-aircraft cannon capable of shooting down fast warplanes. One part of the cannon had to 'perceive' and track an airplane, then calculate its likely trajectory and 'talk' to another part of the cannon to fire the shells. The engineering challenge of this project caused Wiener and some colleagues to create a new branch of science, which Wiener called 'cybernetics'—the science of information feedback systems. The concepts of cybernetics, when combined with the digital computers being created at that time, led Wiener to draw some remarkably insightful ethical conclusions. He perceptively foresaw revolutionary social and ethical consequences. In 1948, for example, in his book *Cybernetics: or Control and Communication in the Animal and the Machine*, he said:

> We are already in a position to construct artificial machines of almost any degree of elaborateness of performance. Long before Nagasaki and the public awareness of the atomic bomb, it had occurred to me that we were here in the presence of another social potentiality of unheard-of importance for good and for evil.

In 1950 Wiener published his monumental book, *The Human Use of Human Beings*, which not only established him as the founder of computer ethics (a term he did not use), but far more importantly, laid down a comprehensive computer ethics foundation which remains today a powerful basis for research and analysis in the field. Wiener made it clear that, in his opinion, the integration of computer technology into society would constitute its remaking—the 'second industrial revolution'—destined to affect every major aspect of life. The computer revolution would be a multi-faceted, ongoing process that would take decades of effort and would radically change everything. Such a vast undertaking would necessarily include a wide diversity of tasks and challenges for workers, governments, professional organisations, sociologists, psychologists and philosophers to deal with.

Unfortunately, this complex and important new area of applied ethics, which Wiener founded in the 1940s, remained nearly undeveloped and unexplored until the mid 1960s. By then, important social and ethical consequences of computer technology had already become manifest, and interest in computer-related ethical issues began to grow. Computer-aided bank robberies and other crimes attracted the attention of Donn Parker, who wrote books and articles on computer crime and created a code of ethics for the members of the Association for Computing Machinery in 1973. (The ACM Code was revised in the early 1980s and again in the early 1990s.)

Also in the mid 1960s, computer-enabled invasions of privacy by 'big-brother' government agencies became a public worry and led to books, articles, government studies, and proposed privacy legislation. By the mid 1970s, new privacy laws and computer crime laws had been enacted in America and in Europe, and organisations of computer professionals were adopting codes of conduct for their members. At the same time, MIT computer scientist Joseph Weizenbaum created a computer program called ELIZA, intended to crudely simulate 'a Rogerian psychotherapist engaged in an initial interview with a patient.' The simple program brought forth a host of appalling reactions Some psychiatrists, for example, viewed his results as evidence that computers will soon provide automated psychotherapy; and certain students and staff at MIT even became emotionally involved with the computer and shared their intimate thoughts with it! Concerned by the ethical implications of such a response, Weizenbaum wrote the book *Computer Power and Human Reason* (1976), which is now considered a classic in computer ethics.

In 1976, while teaching a medical ethics course, Walter Maner noticed that, often, when computers are involved in medical ethics cases, new ethically important considerations arise. This convinced him of the need for a separate branch of applied ethics, which he dubbed 'computer ethics.' Maner defined computer ethics as that branch of applied ethics which studies ethical problems 'aggravated, transformed or created by computer technology' and offered guidelines for dealing with the subject in the classroom in *A Starter Kit for Teaching Computer Ethics*.

Inspired by Maner's work, Terrell Ward Bynum (the writer) developed curriculum materials and a university course in 1979, and in the early 1980s gave speeches and ran workshops at a variety of conferences across America. In 1983, as editor of the journal *Metaphilosophy*, he launched an essay competition to generate interest in computer ethics and to create a special issue of the journal. Entitled 'Computers and Ethics', it was published in 1985 and its lead article—and winner of the essay competition—was James Moor's now-classic essay 'What Is Computer Ethics?', where he described computer ethics.

> Computers provide us with new capabilities and these in turn give us new choices for action. Often, either no policies for conduct in these situations exist or existing policies seem inadequate. A central task of computer ethics is to determine what we should do in such cases. . . Of course, some ethical situations confront us as individuals and some as a society. Computer ethics includes consideration of both personal and social policies for the ethical use of computer technology.

The year 1985 was a watershed year for computer ethics, not only because of the special issue of *Metaphilosophy* and Moor's classic article, but also because Deborah Johnson published the first major textbook in the field, *Computer Ethics*, as well as an edited collection of readings with John Snapper, *Ethical Issues in the Use of Computers*. In her book, Johnson defined computer ethics as a field which examines ways that computers 'pose new versions of standard moral problems and moral dilemmas, exacerbating the old problems, and forcing us to apply ordinary moral norms in uncharted realms.' Unlike Maner (1996), Johnson did not think that computers created wholly new ethical problems, but rather gave a 'new twist' to already familiar issues such as ownership, power, privacy and responsibility.

Since 1985, the field of computer ethics has grown exponentially. New university courses, research centres, conferences, articles and textbooks have appeared, and a wide diversity of additional scholars and topics have become involved. Developments in Europe and Australia have been especially noteworthy, with new research centres being set up in England, Poland, Holland, and Italy and international conferences such as the ETHICOMP series of conferences being organised.

Given the explosive growth of computer ethics during the past two decades, the field appears to have a very robust and significant future. How can it be, then, that two important thinkers —Krystyna Górniak-Kocikowska and Deborah Johnson—have recently argued that computer ethics will disappear as a branch of applied ethics?

In her 1995 ETHICOMP paper, Górniak predicted that computer ethics, which is currently considered just a branch of applied ethics, will evolve into a system of global ethics applicable in every culture on earth.

> Just as the major ethical theories of Bentham and Kant were developed in response to the printing press revolution, so a new ethical theory is likely to emerge from computer ethics in response to the computer revolution. The newly emerging field of information ethics, therefore, is much more important than even its founders and advocates believe.
>
> The very nature of the computer revolution indicates that the ethic of the future will have a global character. It will be global in a spatial sense, since it will encompass the entire globe. It will also be global in the sense that it will address the totality of human actions and relations.

> Computers do not know borders. Computer networks have a truly global character. Hence, when we are talking about computer ethics, we are talking about the emerging global ethic.

According to the Górniak hypothesis, ethical theories of the West and those of other cultures in Asia, Africa, the Pacific Islands, etc., will eventually be superseded by a global ethics evolving from today's computer ethics. 'Computer' ethics, then, will become the 'ordinary' ethics of the information age.

In her 1999 ETHICOMP paper, Deborah Johnson expressed a view which, upon first sight, may seem to be the same as Górniak's.

> I offer you a picture of computer ethics in which computer ethics as such disappears. . . . We will be able to say both that computer ethics has become ordinary ethics and that ordinary ethics has become computer ethics.

But a closer look at the Johnson hypothesis reveals that it is very different from Górniak's. In Górniak's view, the computer revolution will eventually lead to a new ethical system, global and cross-cultural in nature. The new 'ethics for the information age,' according to Górniak, will supplant parochial theories like Bentham's and Kant's based on relatively isolated cultures in Europe, Asia, Africa, and other regions of the globe.

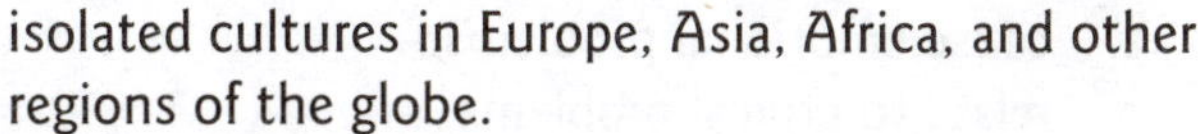

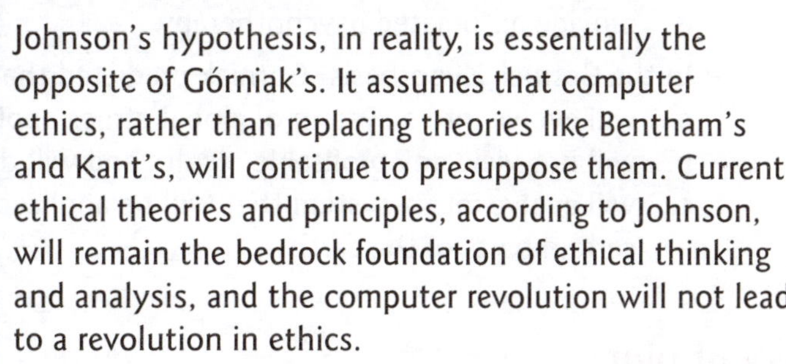

Johnson's hypothesis, in reality, is essentially the opposite of Górniak's. It assumes that computer ethics, rather than replacing theories like Bentham's and Kant's, will continue to presuppose them. Current ethical theories and principles, according to Johnson, will remain the bedrock foundation of ethical thinking and analysis, and the computer revolution will not lead to a revolution in ethics.

At the dawn of the 21st century, then, computer ethics thinkers have offered the world two very different views of the likely ethical relevance of computer technology. The Wiener–Maner–Górniak point of view sees computer technology as ethically revolutionary, requiring human beings to re-examine the foundations of ethics and the very definition of a human life. The more conservative Johnson perspective is that fundamental ethical theories will remain unaffected—that computer ethics issues are simply the same old ethics questions with a new twist—and consequently computer ethics as a distinct branch of applied philosophy will ultimately disappear.

[Adapted from the article 'From the Internet' by Terrell Ward Bynum, published in the Summer 2000 issue of the American Philosophical Association's *Newsletter on Philosophy and Computing*]

Comprehension

A. *Read the given text carefully and answer the following questions briefly.*

1. What do you understand by 'cybernetics'?
2. Why does the computer have 'another social potentiality of unheard-of importance for good and for evil'?
3. How did Wiener think of computer technology as remaking society?
4. How did Maner's work inspire Terrell Bynum?
5. What is your view of the future of computer ethics as derived from this lesson?

B. *Choose from a, b and c the correct endings to the following sentences.*

1. Computer ethics was founded
   a. while setting up a language laboratory.
   b. while helping to develop an anti-aircraft cannon capable of shooting down fast warplanes.
   c. when trying to set up new codes of conduct for organisations.
2. Some psychiatrists viewed Weizenbaum's results as evidence that computers can
   a. cause emotional problems.
   b. relate to ethical problems.
   c. provide automated psychotherapy.
3. In the Gorniak Hypothesis, Gorniak predicted that computer ethics
   a. will evolve into a system of global ethics applicable to every culture on earth.
   b. will not yield any profitable results and will die out.
   c. will evolve into a system that will be applicable only in certain situations and in certain parts of the earth.

Vocabulary

A. *Look at the following words that appear in the text. These hyphenated words are formed by joining a noun and a participle. Think of at least eight words of the same kind.*

computer-aided	computer-generated
computer-enabled	computer-related

B. *The word 'psychotherapist' occurs in the text. The psychotherapist deals with psychotherapy. Say what subjects the following professionionals specialise in.*

paediatrician	astronomer	gynaecologist
psychiatrist	photographer	ophthalmologist
cardiologist	orthopaedist	anaesthetist
obstetrician	neurologist	geriatrician

C. *A synonym is a word that means the same as another word in the same language, e.g. 'tale' and 'story'. Find words in the above text that are synonyms of the following words.*

1. result	2. fated	3. worsen
4. healthy	5. view	6. known

Grammar

You know that nouns have number, that when we talk of one thing we say that the noun is in the singular number and when we talk of more than one thing we say that the noun is in the plural number.

Note how nouns are preceded by articles (*a, an, the*).

Look at the sentences below.

The ostrich is a native of South Africa.
I ate an orange for breakfast.
The orange I ate for breakfast was sweeter than the one I ate for lunchtime.
I saw an ostrich in my garden this morning when I looked out of the window!
It turned out that the ostrich I saw was really a dream.
The dream was a result of over-eating at dinner time.
I have neither ostriches nor gardens. I live in a flat.

Names (proper nouns) are not preceded by an article except in certain cases as in the sentences below.

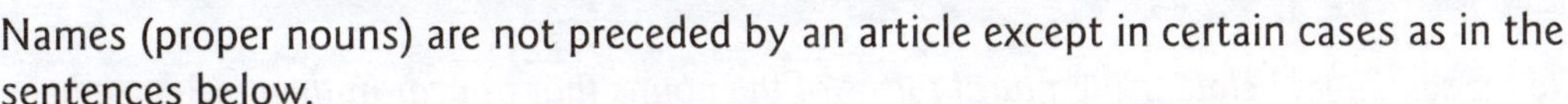

I am talking about the India I knew when I was young.
I look for an India where every child is fed, clothed, sheltered and cared for.

But we do not say:

The France is a European country.

We can say:

We are not talking about ordinary people. We are talking about people like a Shakespeare or a Kalidasa or an Emerson.
The Wordsworth whose poems we studied is not the same as the Wordsworth in your class.

But we do not say:

The Shakespeare wrote plays and sonnets.
or
British live in the England.

Usually only countable nouns take the indefinite article *a/an*. You don't say 'a butter' or 'a ghee' or 'a milk' or 'an oil'. You can of course say:

a packet of butter *or*
a jar of ghee *or*
a glass of milk *or*
a can of oil.

Such uncountable nouns also have no plural—in the mass.
(The plural form is used only when you refer to different kinds of the material, i.e. different kinds of butter may be referred to as 'butters'. So too we may use the plural when we refer to different kinds of oils, e.g. oils are produced and used extensively in India.)

Uncountable nouns (or nouns in the mass) like oil, sugar, water, soil, mud, snow, rain, poetry, prose and so on are not used in the plural.
We may speak of *lumps of mud,* but not *muds*.
Or we may speak of *spoonfuls of sugar* but not *sugars*.
We may speak of *pieces of poetry* (or poems) or of *pieces of prose* but not of *poetries* or *proses*.

Of each pair of sentences below the first sentence is in the plural, the second in the singular.

a. The birds in the cage found their freedom when the cage was opened.
   The bird in the cage found its freedom when the cage was opened.
b. The children know how to swim and are not afraid of water.
   The child knows how to swim and is not afraid of water.

A. *Rewrite the sentences below using plural forms of the nouns that appear in them. (Remember that uncountable nouns have no indefinite article and usually no plural.)*

1. The chair is made of wood.
2. An apple is a fruit.
3. An actor must eat, mustn't he?
4. A bee lives in a hive.
5. A shopping bag can be useful.
6. The river was flooded.
7. Ink is available in this store.
8. The child eats rice.

B. *Rewrite the sentences below using singular forms of the nouns that appear in them. (Remember to use the article wherever necessary.)*

1. The women knitted mufflers for the soldiers.
2. We drank cups of tea and ate biscuits.
3. Rocking chairs are comfortable pieces of furniture.
4. Elephants are intelligent animals.
5. Dodos are extinct.
6. Fools rush in where angels fear to tread.
7. Babies need care.
8. Elves are fairy creatures that appear in old stories.

C. *Rewrite the sentences below putting in 'a,' 'an,' 'the' or 'some' where necessary.*

1. There was once .... beggar who lived in .... capital city of .... king's great empire.
2. .... atlas will show you the location of .... cities you are looking for.
3. Have you seen .... Amitabh Bachchan's .... latest film?
4. I have .... milk and .... slice of cake for you.
5. There's .... ghost we saw yesterday again. Can you see it?
6. .... people are friendly while others are not.

D. *Change the plural nouns in the sentences below into singular nouns and rewrite the sentences. (Remember to use the appropriate indefinite article, a/an.)*

1. Planets revolve round their suns.
2. The sheep and oxen were great friends.
3. Will you lend us books?
4. The children sang songs to entertain us.
5. The students wrote letters to their parents.

Listening

Your teacher will play to you numbered words on tape, each spoken twice. For each word that you listen to, you will find a set of printed meanings below. Tick the meaning that corresponds to the spoken word.

A. 1. the part of the land adjoining the sea
   2. a marine mollusc with a spiral shell
   3. a railway carriage
   4. an upholstered piece of furniture

B. 1. allocate a task to somebody
   2. to give one's approval
   3. to sign on a document
   4. to accept as true without proof

C. 1. put forward
   2. drive or push forward
   3. fulfil
   4. force somebody to do something

D. 1. not false
   2. some
   3. made something move through air
   4. made a picture or diagram on paper

E. 1. soft, chalk rock
2. peaceful and undisturbed
3. fill to the point of overflowing
4. soothing ointment for the skin

F. 1. no longer fresh
2. a booth for the sale of goods in a market
3. a dirty mark
4. take something without permission and without intending to return it

Speaking

Listen to the dialogue that your teacher will play for you on tape and also read its transcript in your book. Pay attention to the italicised expressions in the transcript. The dialogue, which presents a situation where two people introduce themselves to each other, occurs in a formal situation, but the same expressions can be used in an informal situation as well except for those used to greet and take leave of each other (refer to unit 1).

Dialogue 1 (formal)

(Mrs Shakti Thomas walks up to Mr Abhay Sarkar, an employee in the bank where she has just started work.)

Mrs Thomas: *Good morning! I'm Shakti Thomas. I've joined the bank today as an assistant accounts officer. I was with a private finance company in Trichy earlier.*

Mr Sarkar (rising to his feet): *Good morning! I'm happy to meet you. I'm Abhay Sarkar, and I'm a manager in the housing loans division. Welcome to our bank!*

Mrs Thomas: *Thank you, Mr Sarkar. Very nice meeting you too.*

Exercise A

You will now hear on tape some expressions used in both formal and informal situations to introduce yourself to somebody. Listen to each item and repeat it with a name of your choice.

1. Good morning!/Hello! My name is ....
2. Good morning!/Hi! I'm ....
3. I have just joined ....
4. I have just moved in ....
5. I'm from ....
6. I work for ....
7. I'm the new ....

Listen to another two dialogues that your teacher will play for you on tape and also read their transcripts in your book. Pay attention to the italicised expressions in the transcripts of the dialogues presenting situations where a person introduces two other people to each other. The first dialogue occurs in a formal situation while the second occurs in an informal one.

Dialogue 2 (formal)

(Dr Preeta Rao and Mr Salil Mohammad meet for the first time at the workplace of a common friend, Mrs Padma Padamsee.)

Mrs Padamsee: *Dr Rao, I'd like to introduce you to Mr Salil Mohammad. Mr Mohammad is our company secretary. Mr Mohammad, please meet Dr Preeta Rao. Dr Rao is an educational advisor with the UNICEF.*

Dr Rao *(shaking hands): How d'you do, Mr Mohammad? I'm happy to meet you.*

Mr Mohammad: *Thank you, Dr Rao. This is indeed a pleasure. Mrs Padamsee has spoken to me about the fine work that you are doing among children in government schools.*

Dialogue 3 (informal)

(Kritika introduces her sister Alka to her classmate John.)

Kritika: *John, this is my sister, Alka. She's an editor with the* Times of India. *Alka, meet John. He's my classmate and captain of the college basketball team.*

John: *Hi, Alka! Nice meeting you.*

Alka: *Hello, John. It's nice meeting you too.* I used to know your cousin, Stella at the K. N. Degree College.

Exercise B

You will now hear on tape some expressions used in formal and in informal situations to introduce two persons to each other and those that they can use to respond. Listen to each item and repeat it filling in a name of your choice.

1. I'd like to introduce you to ....
2. Please meet ....
3. This is ....
4. ...., meet ....
5. I'm happy to meet you.
6. This is indeed a pleasure.
7. Nice meeting you.

Exercise C

Working first in pairs and then in a group of three, write and enact the following situations in the form of brief dialogues choosing appropriate expressions from those given above.

1. Rohit Kumar from Alpha Electronics, Kanpur, enters the Delhi office of his company's chartered accountant with whom he has an appointment. He introduces himself to the person's secretary, explaining who he is, where he is from and why he is there.
2. Dharam goes to his friend Praveen's house. His cousin, Smita, is with him. Dharam introduces the two to each other.

Writing

Essay writing

Some useful points to remember

- The essay is a long piece of composition on a theme or subject.
- Essays are of different types depending on whether they describe, narrate, inform or present arguments to convince the reader about a particular opinion.
- An essay must have unity of theme, which means that you should have your aim clearly set down before you start writing.
- You can give emphasis to the main idea in the essay by placing it in a prominent position (for example, the beginning or end), either by giving more space to it or by directly stating it.
- The beginning introduces the subject of the essay, the middle develops the theme and the concluding paragraph(s) take it to a suitable close.
- To ensure that your essay has the quality of balance, the points that are included in it must be given the treatment they deserve according to their importance. For example, avoid making your introduction so long that there is a delay in your getting to the main point.
- For an essay to be coherent, arrange the ideas it contains in a definite order and also make clear the link between any two adjacently placed points.
- An essay should not be loosely structured or rambling, and every part should contribute to its total meaning.
- Most essays are written in a formal style. Thus, complete sentences are used and colloquial expressions and slang are avoided.

Following the steps in the figure below will help you in writing a well-developed essay.

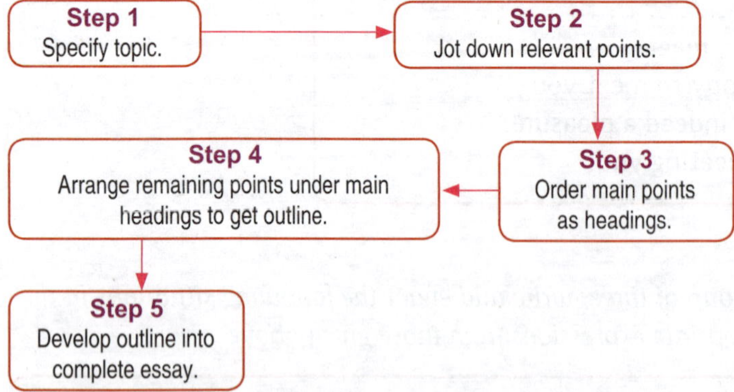

Look at the following outline of an essay on machine civilisation for an illustration of the actual steps you can take in writing one of your own.

A. Features of machine civilisation

   1. short historical note.

a. Industrial Revolution to early 19th century
b. late 19th century and 20th century
2. machines and modern industry
3. machines in daily life
4. machines have made the world smaller
a. faster travel
b. faster communication

B. Advantages of machine civilisation
1. higher standard of living
a. luxuries and comforts
b. abundance
2. faster travel: by land, air or sea
3. leisure and entertainment
a. radio, cinema, television
b. books and magazines

C. Disadvantages of machine civilisation
1. quality of life has fallen: life has become mechanical
2. pollution
3. noise
4. craze for speed
5. dependence on machines

After writing an essay, always read through your draft and revise it, paying attention to clarity and grammatical accuracy.

Exercises

A. *Write an essay on the benefits of meditation. You can get the required information from books in your college library or find it on the Internet.*

B. *You will find below some commonly held views on bandhs. Think about the issue, take a stand and write an essay expressing your attitude to bandhs.*

A student leader: I think a bandh is the only way people can show their protest when the government makes arbitrary decisions.

A doctor: This is not democracy. A few people, sometimes rowdies engaged by politicians, force others to join the bandh against their will.

A headmistress: Our students have already lost four working days.

A political leader: The bandh has the support of the people. They are fed up with the government's policies.

A parent: No politician cares for the common person. We can't go to work, our children miss school, people miss interviews and important meetings, and why, we can't even reach a hospital in an emergency!

An industrialist: When there is a bandh, one day's work is lost. This would put back our economy by several points.

A union leader: A bandh represents a Gandhian way of standing together against injustice.

C. *Write an essay on the topic 'The problem of city slums and possible humane solutions'. (Visit a library or use the Internet for information and views on the subject. Your teacher could help you organise your class into groups and hold a discussion. List the points that come up and make an outline with main points, sub- and sub-subpoints. Finally expand the outline into an essay.)*

Language games

Two trains have derailed, and their numbered coaches, starting with the engine, all lie scattered about. Search among each jumble of coaches and number them in ascending order. Connect with punctuation marks and use capital letters where necessary to rebuild the train.

1. [it will be] ○ [to define] ○

   [to bring out] ○ [the interview system] ○

   [if] ○ [what sort of students] ○

   [necessary for universities] ○ [is to continue] ○

   [they wish] ○ [much more precisely] ○

2. [major threat] ○ [of the world] ○

   [two billion people] ○ [because of it] ○ [including India] ○

   [in many parts] ○ [water scarcity] ○ [with] ○

   [is a] ○ [dying] ○

Travel
and
Transport

THE CLIMB TO ANNAPURNA

I felt as though I were plunging into something new and quite abnormal. I had the strangest and most vivid impressions, such as I had never before known in the mountains. There was something unnatural in the way I saw Lachenal and everything round us. I smiled to myself at the paltriness of our efforts, for I could stand apart and watch myself making these efforts. But all sense of exertion was gone, as though there were no longer any gravity. This diaphanous landscape, this quintessence of purity—these were not the mountains I knew; they were the mountains of my dreams.

The snow, sprinkled over every rock and gleaming in the sun, was of a radiant beauty that touched me to the heart. I had never seen such complete transparency; I was living in a world of crystal. Sounds were indistinct, the atmosphere like cotton wool.

An astonishing happiness welled up in me, but I could not define it. Everything was so new, so utterly unprecedented. It was not in the least like anything I had known in the Alps, where one feels buoyed up by the presence of others—by people of whom one is vaguely aware, or even by the dwellings one can see in the far distance.

This was quite different. An enormous gulf was between me and the world. This was a different universe—withered, desert, lifeless; a fantastic universe where the presence of man was not foreseen, perhaps not desired. We were braving an interdict, overstepping a boundary, and yet we had no fear as we continued upwards. I thought of the famous ladder of St Theresa of Avila. Something clutched at my heart.

Did Lachenal share these feelings? The summit ridge drew nearer and we reached the foot of the ultimate rock band. The slope was steep and the snow interspersed with rocks.

'Couloir!'

A finger pointed. The whispered word from one to another indicated the key to the rocks—the last line of defence.

'What luck!'

The couloir up the rocks, though steep, was feasible.

The sky was always a deep sapphire blue. With a great effort we made over to the right, avoiding the rocks; we preferred to keep to the snow on account of our crampons and it was not long before we set foot in the couloir. It was fairly steep, and we had a minute's hesitation. Should we have enough strength left to overcome this final obstacle?

Fortunately the snow was hard, and by kicking steps we were able to manage, thanks to our crampons. A false move would have been fatal. There was no need to make handholds—our axes, driven in as far as possible, served us for an anchor

Lachenal went splendidly. What a wonderful contrast to the early days! It was a hard struggle here, but he kept going. Lifting our eyes occasionally from the slope, we saw the couloir opening out on to—well, we didn't quite know, probably a ridge. But where was the top—left or right? Stopping at every step, leaning on our axes, we tried to recover our breath and to calm down our hearts, which were thumping as though they would burst. We knew we were there now, and that no difficulty could stop us. No need to exchange looks—each of us would have read the same determination in the other's eyes. A slight detour to the left, a few more steps—the summit ridge came gradually nearer—a few rocks to avoid. We dragged ourselves up. Could we possibly be there?

Yes!

A fierce and savage wind tore at us.

We were on top of Annapurna! 8,075 metres, 26,493 feet.

Our hearts overflowed with an unspeakable happiness.

'If only the others could know...'

If only everyone could know!

The summit was a corniced crest of ice, and the precipices on the far side, which plunged vertically down beneath us, were terrifying, unfathomable. There could be few other mountains in the world like this. Clouds floated half way down, concealing the gentle, fertile valley of Pokhara, 23,000 feet below. Above us there was nothing!

Our mission was accomplished. But at the same time we had accomplished something infinitely greater. How wonderful life would now become! What an inconceivable experience it is to attain one's ideal and, at the very same moment, to fulfil oneself. I was stirred to the depths of my being. Never had I felt happiness like this—so intense and yet so pure. That brown rock, the highest of them all, that ridge of ice—were these the goals of a lifetime? Or were they, rather, the limits of man's pride?

'Well, what about going down?

Lachenal shook me. What were his own feelings? Did he simply think he had finished another climb, as in the Alps? Did he think one could just go down again like that, with nothing more to it?

'One minute, I must take some photographs.'

'Hurry up!'

I fumbled feverishly in my sack, pulled out the camera, took out the little French flag which was right at the bottom, and the pennants. Useless gestures, no doubt, but something more than symbols—eloquent tokens of affection and goodwill. I tied the strips of material—stained by sweat and by the food in the sacks—to the shaft of my ice-axe, the only flag-staff at hand. Then I focused my camera on Lachenal.

'Now, will you take me?'

'Hand it over—hurry up!' said Lachenal.

He took several pictures and then handed me back the camera. I loaded a colour-film and we repeated the process to be certain of bringing back records to be cherished in the future.

'Are you mad?' asked Lachenal. 'We haven't a minute to lose: we must go down at once.'

And in fact a glance round showed me that the weather was no longer gloriously fine as it had been in the morning. Lachenal was becoming impatient.

'We must go down!'

He was right. His was the reaction of the mountaineer who knows his own domain. But I just could not accustom myself to the idea that we had won our victory. It seemed inconceivable that we should have trodden those summit snows.

It was impossible to build a cairn; there were no stones, and everything was frozen. Lachenal stamped his feet; he felt them freezing. I felt mine freezing too, but paid little attention. The highest mountain to be climbed by man lay under our feet! The names of our predecessors on these heights chased each other through my mind: Mummery, Mallory and Irvine, Bauer, Welzenbach, Tilman, Shipton. How many of them were dead—how many had found on these mountains what, to them, was the finest end of all?

My joy was touched with humility. It was not just one party that had climbed Annapurna today, but a whole expedition. I thought of all the others in the camps perched on the slopes at our feet, and I knew it was because of their efforts and their sacrifices that we had succeeded today. There are times when the most complex actions are suddenly summed up, distilled, and strike you with illuminating clarity: so it was with this irresistible upward surge which had landed us two here.

Pictures passed through my mind—the Chamonix valley, where I had spent the most marvellous moments of my childhood, Mont Blanc, which so tremendously impressed me! I was a child when I first saw 'the Mont Blanc people' coming home, and to me there was a queer look about them; a strange light shone in their eyes.

'Come on, straight down,' called Lachenal.

He had already done up his sack and started going down. I took out my pocket aneroid: 8,500 metres. I smiled. I swallowed a little condensed milk and left the tube behind—the only trace of our passage. I did up my sack, put on my gloves and my glasses, seized my ice-axe; one look round and I, too, hurried down the slope. Before disappearing into the couloir I gave one last look at the summit which would henceforth be all our joy and all our consolation.

Lachenal was already far below; he had reached the foot of the couloir. I hurried down in his tracks. I went as fast as I could, but it was dangerous going. At every step one had to take care that the snow did not break away beneath one's weight. Lachenal, going faster than I thought he was capable of, was now on the long traverse. It was my turn to cross the area of mixed rock and snow. At last I reached the foot of the rock-band. I had hurried and I was out of breath. I undid my sack. What had I been going to do? I could not say.

'My gloves!'

Before I had time to bend over, I saw them slide and roll. They went further and further straight down the slope. I remained where I was, quite stunned. I watched them rolling down slowly, with no appearance of stopping. The movement of those gloves was engraved in my sight as something ineluctable, irremediable, against which I was powerless. The consequences might be most serious. What was I to do?

'Quickly, down to Camp V.'

Rebuffat and Terray should be there. My concern dissolved like magic. I now had a fixed objective again: to reach the camp. Never for a minute did it occur to me to use as gloves the socks which I always carry in reserve for just such a mishap as this.

On I went, trying to catch up with Lachenal. It had been two o'clock when we reached the summit; we had started out at six in the morning; but I had to admit that I had lost all sense of time. I felt as if I were running, whereas in actual fact I was walking normally, perhaps rather slowly, and I had to keep stopping to get my breath. The sky was now covered with clouds, everything had become grey and dirty-looking. An icy wind sprang up, boding no good. We must push on! But where was Lachenal? I spotted him a couple of hundred yards away, looking as if he was never going to stop. And I had thought he was in indifferent form!

The clouds grew thicker and came right down over us; the wind blew stronger, but I did not suffer from the cold. Perhaps the descent had restored my circulation. Should I be able to find the tents in the mist? I watched the rib ending in the beak-like point which overlooked the camp. It was gradually swallowed up by the clouds, but I was able to make out the spearhead rib lower down. If the mist should thicken I would make straight for that rib and follow it down, and in this way I should be bound to come upon the tent.

Lachenal disappeared from time to time, and then the mist was so thick that I lost sight of him altogether. I kept going at the same speed, as fast as my breathing would allow.

The slope was now steeper; a few patches of bare ice followed the smooth stretches of snow. A good sign—I was nearing the camp. How difficult to find one's way in thick mist! I kept the course which I had set by the steepest angle of the slope. The ground was broken; with my crampons I went straight down walls of bare ice. There were some patches ahead—a few

more steps. It was the camp all right, but there were two tents.

So Rebuffat and Terray had come up. What a mercy! I should be able to tell them that we had been successful, that we were returning from the top. How thrilled they would be!

I got there, dropping down from above. The platform had been extended, and the two tents were facing each other. I tripped over one of the guy-ropes of the first tent; there was movement inside—they had heard me. Rebuffat and Terray put their heads out.

'We've made it. We're back from Annapurna!'

[From Maurice Harzog, *Annapurna: Conquest of the first 8000-metre peak*, translated from French by Nea Morin and Janet Adam Smith, 1952]

Comprehension

Choose from a, b, c, d and e the correct endings to the following sentences.

1. Once the decision was made that he would climb to the top alone if need be, the mountain climber felt as if
   a. everything was worthless and meaningless.
   b. a strange happiness such as he had never felt before.
   c. as if the landscape was made of cotton wool.
   d. frightened.
   e. a sense of responsibility.
2. When he had climbed the Alps in the past
   a. he had felt as if he was a ship at sea.
   b. he had been less scared and unhappy.
   c. he had felt cheered up by the sight of other people and of houses and villages in the distance.
   d. he had felt as if he was climbing a ladder.
   e. he had never dreamed it was going to be so beautiful.
3. Lachenal who was a real mountaineer
   a. wanted to take photographs to show his friends.
   b. knew the dangers of staying even a minute too long on the mountain top.
   c. was an ill-tempered man.
   d. thought of all the great mountain climbers who had conquered Annapurna.
   e. thought his friend was mad.
4. The writer of this account
   a. was powerless to stop his gloves as they rolled down the mountain.
   b. threw down his gloves.
   c. was really careless and inexperienced.
   d. was frozen to death on the mountain.
   e. said goodbye to Lachenal.

5. The writer of this account
   a. did not remember to wear his socks.
   b. left his things behind on the top of the mountain.
   c. wanted to reach the camp before he froze to death.
   d. disappeared in the couloir and was never found again.
   e. always wore socks, shoes and gloves.

Vocabulary

Below are words from the text with their meanings. Use the correct words to fill in the blanks in the short passages below.

unfathomable:	what cannot be understood or guessed
fumble:	move your fingers or hands awkwardly when you are looking for something or doing something
feasible:	possible to do
convince:	make someone believe something
to be buoyed up:	to be cheered up or made lighter in spirit
anchor:	a heavy hooked metal object that is dropped into the water to keep a boat from moving away
detour:	a way of going from one place to another which is longer than the usual way
humility:	the quality of being humble, i.e. without pride or arrogance.
diaphanous:	thin and almost transparent
irresistible:	what cannot be fought back; what you cannot stop yourself from accepting or doing

1. First she lost her job. Then her father broke his knee and had to be in plaster and finally her son failed his exam. Everything was going wrong; nothing was going right. For a day Vanita was thoroughly depressed. But her natural optimism and capacity for laughter .... until better times returned.
2. We made many plans for the journey, but none of them was .... and so we had to give them up.
3. We arrived very late. The road was being repaired and was closed. So we had to make a .... and that took us several kilometres out of our way and delayed us.
4. I had to eat. The food on the table looked too tempting. It was quite .... and I broke my fast and had soon eaten a full meal.
5. He has left his home and gone into the mountains to live. When asked for an explanation he says nothing. I have tried to understand him but the reasons for his strange behaviour are quite .... and I have given up.
6. What impressed us about the president who had won so many honours was his .... He never boasted, never insisted on giving his opinion; he always made room for others and listened respectfully to them.

7. At the back of the stage they had hung curtains of .... cloth through which we could see the dance. It gave the effect of fairylands that was almost magical.
8. When the ticket collector came and asked for the tickets, she put her fingers into her purse and .... for it. She could not find it because it was in her box.
9. As long as the grandmother was alive she held the family together and the boy came to her for advice and help. But after she died he was like a boat without an .... and seemed quite lost.
10. I spoke to my friend for over an hour about the advantages of living in the USA but I couldn't .... him.

Grammar

Prepositions are frequently used words that show a connection or relation between a verb and a noun, a noun and a pronoun or a noun and a noun. (They are also words which are frequently misused!). They need to be used correctly and with care. Some prepositions are:

at, to, in, on, into, above, below, from, over, behind, between, beside, before, beneath, through, against, across, inside, outside, out of, up, down, under, since

A. *Fill in the blanks with suitable prepositions.*

1. The secret .... success lies ...hard work.
2. Mr Sethi lives .... an apartment building in Punjagutta.
3. Since the old man was hard .... hearing, I had to speak very loudly to him.
4. Sita reminded me .... my appointment with the doctor.
5. The President congratulated him .... his splendid victory.
6. The workers complained .... their low wages and asked for more.
7. I must apologise .... you for not recognising you at the party.

B. *Fill in the blanks in the passage below with the correct prepositions from the above list.*

.... the evenings the old man would sit .... the wooden bench .... the yard, and his wife would sit .... him. The little boy took his seat .... the two of them. The child had sat thus every evening ever .... he could remember. .... him was the endless sky and .... him the brown earth. Sometimes the child would lean .... his grandmother as he looked up .... the birds perched ......

the branches .... the old tamarind tree. That tree had been there as long as the village had been there. .... the distance came the muezzin's call to prayer. It was a peaceful existence .... those far-off days.

We use a singular verb with a singular noun and a plural verb with a plural noun in the simple present tense. For example,

A student wants to see you.

Students want to see you.

With an uncountable noun we usually use a singular verb in the simple present tense. For example,

Water freezes at 0 degrees centigrade.

The main verb does not change at all in the simple past tense. For example,

From that time on, I became your devoted friend.

Similarly, the main verb does not change at all in the simple future tense. For example,

From now on, I shall become your devoted friend.

C. *Fill in the blanks with either the singular or the plural form of the verbs in brackets according to the tense indicated in the brackets.*

1. My son .... in class 7. (study: simple present)
2. My neighbours .... their radio loudly. (play: simple present)
3. The books that you bought me .... on the table. (lie: present continuous)
4. The man whom you met at the station.......... to see you. (want: simple present)
5. The girl whose mother gave you a gift .... for you in the common room. (wait: present continuous)
6. It .... when I left for work. (rain: past continuous)
7. The mice in the attic .... a nuisance. (be: simple past)
8. The children .... for you at school. (wait: past continuous)
9. We .... in a hotel when we go there. (stay: simple future)
10. The bell .... at 9 a.m. (ring: simple future)

Listening

A. *Listen to the words played for you on the tape by your teacher. For each word, indicate the syllable that is stressed by placing the accent mark(') in front of it in the corresponding printed word below (as, for example, in pre'vent).*

1. baggage	5. defect
2. demand	6. register
3. fifteen	7. understand
4. possess	8. disappoint

B. *Listen to your teacher play four sets of words on tape. Indicate the stressed syllables in each case by placing the accent mark(') in front of it in the corresponding words given below.*

1.	2.	3.	4.
democrat	demonstrate	photograph	bacteria
democracy	demonstrative	photographer	bacteriology
democratic	demonstration	photographic	bacteriological

Speaking

Listen to the dialogues that your teacher will play for you on tape and also read their transcripts in your book. Pay attention to the italicised expressions in the transcripts. The dialogues present situations where requests are made for help, to seek directions, etc.

Dialogue 1 (formal)

(Vikram is filling in a form at a railway booking counter when his pen stops writing. He turns to a stranger standing next to him and requests her to lend him a pen.)

Vikram: *I'm sorry to bother you, but I need your help.*
My pen is not writing. *May I borrow yours, please?*

Stranger: *Certainly.* Here, you can use this pen.

Vikram *(uses the pen and returns it to its owner):*
I've completed filling in the form. *Thank you very much!*

Stranger: *You're welcome!*

Dialogue 2 (informal)

(Vimala asks her friend Aman if he could get an application form from the passport office.)

Vimala: Aman, *could you do me a favour, please. I'd like you to pick up a passport application form for me on your way back from office.*

Aman: *Sure, I'll do that today.*

Vimala: *Hope it won't be a problem.*

Aman: *Of course not! No problem at all.*

Vimala: *Thanks!*

Aman: *Not at all.*

Dialogue 3 (formal)

(Lata is on her way to her friend's office and has lost her way. She stops a passerby and asks for directions.)

Lata: *Excuse me, please. Could you tell me how to get to Kedarpuri junction, please.*

Passerby: *Certainly, just go straight ahead and then take the second turning to your left. Drive on until you see a children's park. Turn right and then right again and you'll find yourself at the Kedarpuri junction. Have you understood?*

Lata: *Yes, that shouldn't be difficult to find. Thank you very much.*

Passerby: *You're welcome.*

Exercise A

You will now hear on tape some expressions used in both formal and informal situations to make requests and also to respond to them. Listen to each item and repeat it, using the right intonation.

- Do you think I could use your telephone, please?
- Could I ask a favour of you?
- Excuse me, could you help me, please.
- I'm sorry to trouble you, but I need your help.
- Would you mind helping me with this, please?
- I wonder if you could do me a favour.
- Certainly, I shall be glad to help.
- Sure. I'd be glad to help.
- Of course, by all means.
- Thank you.
- Thank you very much.
- Thanks a lot.
- You're most welcome.
- You're welcome.
- Not at all.

Exercise B

Working in pairs, write and enact the following situations in the form of brief dialogues choosing appropriate expressions from those given above.

1. Mr Joseph has just arrived in Guntur and asks a traffic policeman for directions to a hotel where his office has made arrangements for his stay.
2. Chandra requests her neighbour, Madhu, to teach her to bake a cake.
3. Priya goes to the head of her department with a request for a day's leave.

Writing

Writing business letters

Some useful points to remember

- A business letter is written to communicate with somebody on an official or business matter.
- The business letter also differs from the personal letter in its form.
- While the style of writing a business letter is formal, the use of a stiff, impersonal style is no longer followed.
- It is important to be courteous and considerate for you would want to get a friendly response from the person who will read your letter.
- A business letter should be precise and clear. State clearly what you want to know or what you are ordering or offering.
- A business letter must be complete with regard to all the information that may be required by the person or organisation you are writing to.
- Business letters should be brief. State your reason for writing in the opening paragraph. Give the actual message in the middle paragraph(s) and refer to the action expected of the addressee in the closing paragraph.

Figure (a) on page 43 will give you at a glance the components found in a business letter. Note, however, that the items in parentheses do not always appear in such letters.

Modern business correspondence makes use of three formats: the block style, the modified block style and the modified semi-block style that you see in the figure (b) on page 44. Of these, the block style is the one that is most commonly used now.

Exercises

A. *Pramila David has arrived in Delhi on transfer and needs a telephone connection. Write a letter of application for Pramila, addressed to the General Manager, Bharat Sanchar Nigam Limited, Hauz Khas, New Delhi 110 016.*

B. *You are the sports secretary of your college. Write a letter to Sportsman's Paradise, Kalbadevi, Mumbai, asking for a trade catalogue. Mention the items you intend to buy and ask for a discount on the catalogue price.*

C. *Imagine that the manager of the National Dairy Project near your town has invited your class to visit the milk chilling and bottling plant. Write a letter as written by your class secretary thanking him for the invitation, giving him the date and time of the visit and the number of students in the group and telling him what you would particularly like to see.*

D. *You are a student in the first year of BA (economics) at the R. P. Memorial College, Hyderabad. Your brother, who has completed his training, is shortly going to be commissioned as an officer in the Indian army. Write a letter to your principal requesting him/her to grant you three days' leave so that you could be present at your brother's passing-out ceremony at the National Defence Academy, Kharakwasla.*

E. *Write a letter of application in reply to any one of the following advertisements.*

Wanted an experienced office assistant with good knowledge of English, Hindi and Telugu. Contact Box No. 9876, c/o The Deccan Chronicle, Hyderabad 500 001.

Wanted a chef with at least five years' experience in 3-star hotels, for immediate appointment. Must be able to take full charge of kitchen supervision. Apply Hotel Astor, Kolkata 700 001.

Students! Earn your pocket money during the holidays. Door-to-door consumer survey and canvassing for fast-moving cosmetic items. Only for residents of Nagpur. Apply Box No. 4567, c/o Nagpur Chronicle, Nagpur 440 001.

* * *

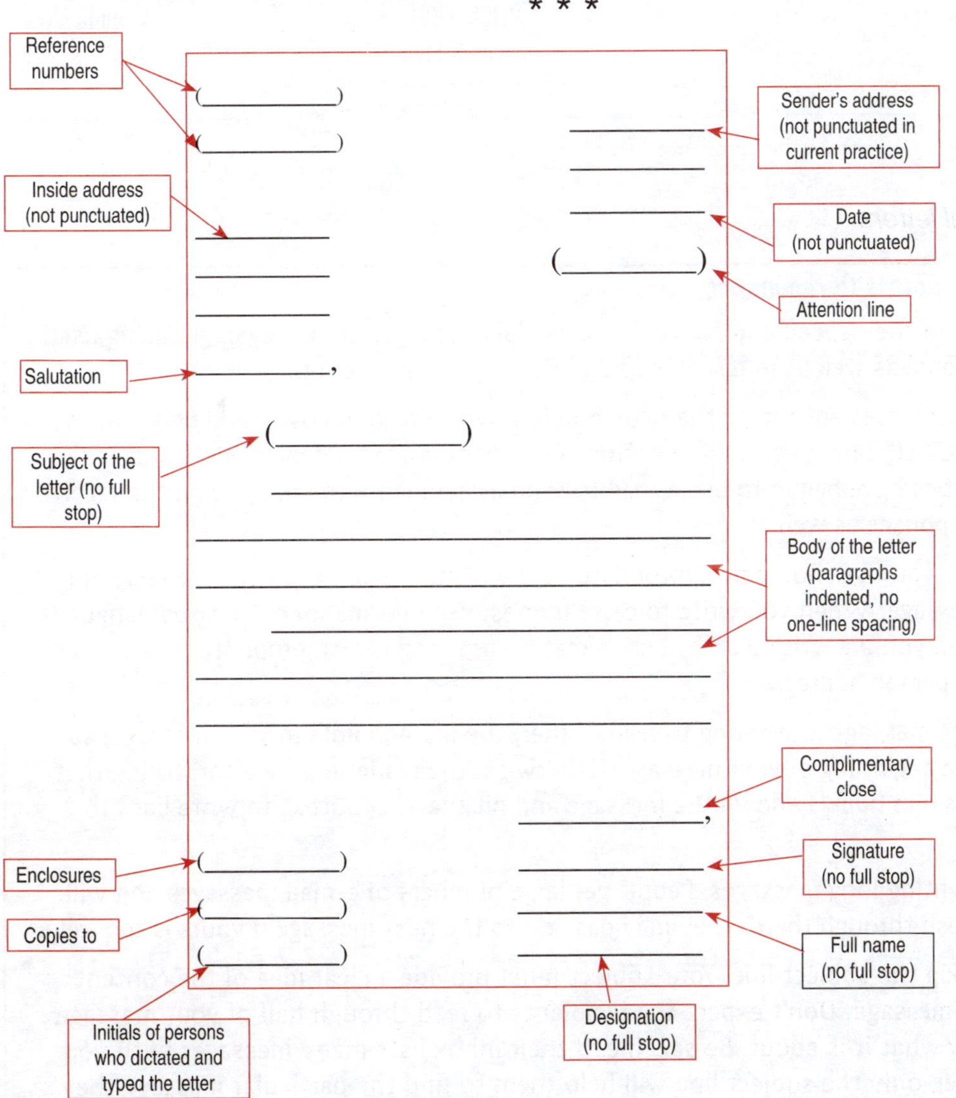

Fig. (a)

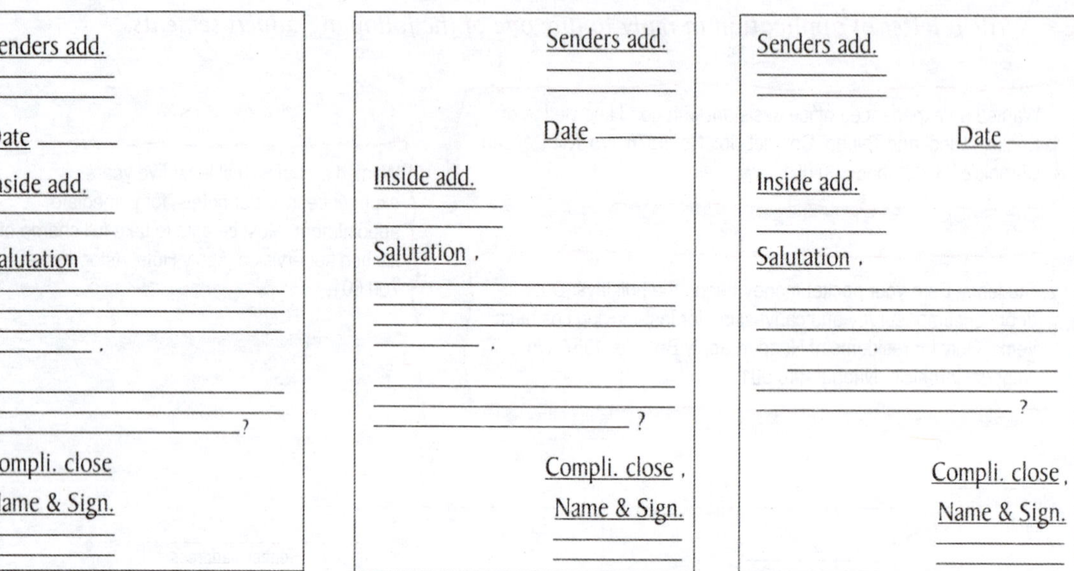

Fig. (b)

Writing e-mail letters

Some useful points to remember

- Because of their speed and convenience, e-mail messages are increasingly being used for personal as well as in research and business communication.
- Most businesses encourage their customers to write to them by providing a CONTACT US button on their website. Also, many research departments and universities have begun to use e-mail to send assignments to students and to receive their responses as well.
- The tone you use should be appropriate to the relation you have with the recipient of your message. When you write to close friends, use informal or even casual language. But when you are writing on a serious matter, use language appropriate to the topic and the person addressed.
- Make the message interesting to read. If there are many points in your message, say so at the beginning of your message. Otherwise, the reader may see something that interests him halfway down the message and hit the REPLY button to write back to you.
- Avoid writing long messages. People get large numbers of e-mail messages and will try to rush through them. They may pass on to the next message if yours is too long.
- Don't skip the subject line. Your subject must provide a clear idea of the content of your message. Don't expect the recipients to read through half of your message to know what it is about. Be specific. If their inbox lists many messages with you as sender, only the subject line will help them to find the particular message they want to locate.

- Be careful when sending attachments. Send them only if necessary. Attachments can take a long time to download, especially with graphics or photographs in them; they can carry viruses; and they can be incompatible with the software of the recipient's computer.
- Don't use e-mail messages to attack someone or to vent your anger. Typing the whole message in capital letters is considered to be a rude act, known as 'flaming'. The recipient may take offence at it.
- Don't write anything in your message which may be illegal or unethical. Though e-mail affords privacy to users, remember that anything that you send can be retrieved by hackers, by your employers or by government investigating agencies and even by criminals.
- Be careful about sending copies to others. Avoid typing a list of fifty addresses in the cc line (which identifies the people who get copies). Use the bcc (blind copy) line for people who want to keep their privacy.

Here is a specimen e-mail message.

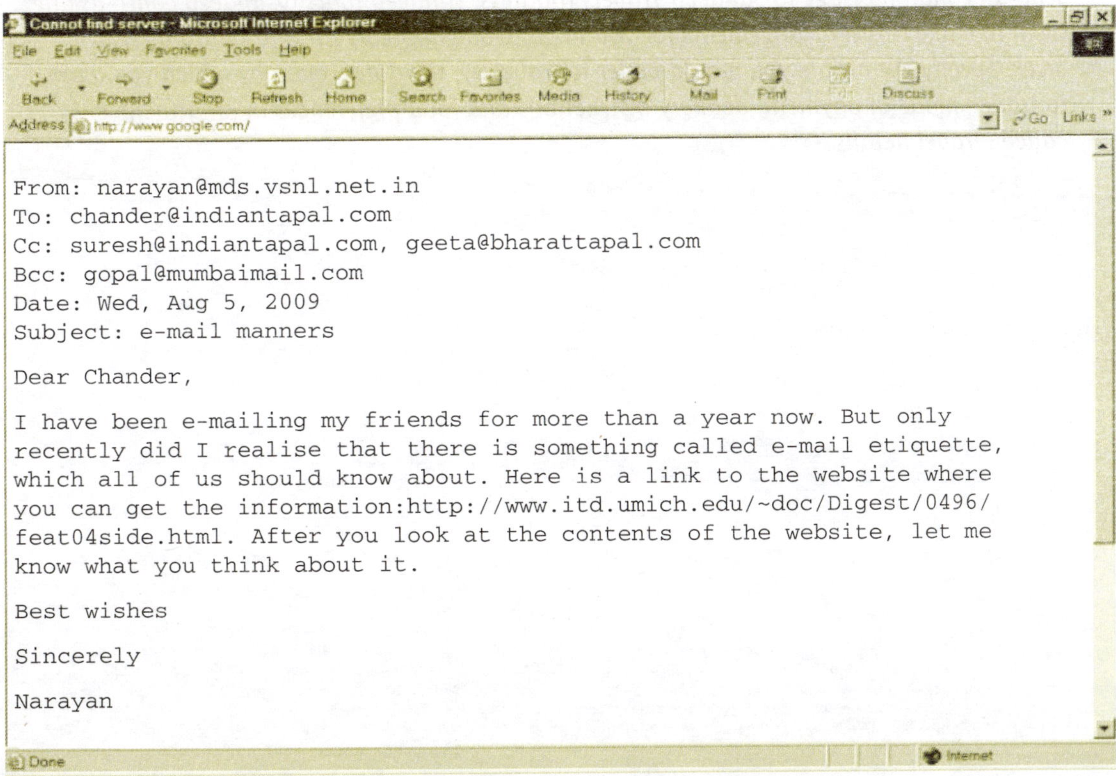

From: narayan@mds.vsnl.net.in
To: chander@indiantapal.com
Cc: suresh@indiantapal.com, geeta@bharattapal.com
Bcc: gopal@mumbaimail.com
Date: Wed, Aug 5, 2009
Subject: e-mail manners

Dear Chander,

I have been e-mailing my friends for more than a year now. But only recently did I realise that there is something called e-mail etiquette, which all of us should know about. Here is a link to the website where you can get the information:http://www.itd.umich.edu/~doc/Digest/0496/feat04side.html. After you look at the contents of the website, let me know what you think about it.

Best wishes

Sincerely

Narayan

Note the structure of the e-mail letter, which has the following components.

From. The sender of the message will type his or her e-mail address here.

To. Here you can type the e-mail address of the recipient; more than one address can be written, separated by commas.

Cc (carbon copy, or copy to). Here you type a list of addresses to which you want to send copies of your message.

Bcc (blind carbon copy). The recipients' addresses, which you type here, will not be seen by other recipients. Use this if the addressee likes to keep his or her privacy.

Subject. Here you type the subject of the message. Don't leave this blank; give a specific title that will help the recipient to know what the message is about.

Attachments. These are files which go with your message. The recipient has to download them in order to read or see them.

Exercises

A. The New Observer, *a newspaper, has invited readers to send letters to the editor to the e-mail address, letters@newobserver.com. Write an e-mail letter saying that their report on a seminar held in your town was misleading. The report had said that the seminar ended in confusion and disorderly behaviour by two groups of participants, which is not true.*

B. *You have to go to Singapore to work on a software project for your company in Bangalore. Send an e-mail message to Sandeep Travels (address: sandeep tours@sandeep.com), asking them to make travel arrangements for you to go to Singapore by air and return after a week. Specify the airline you would prefer to travel by, the dates, class by which you want to travel, mode of payment, delivery instructions and food preferences in an attachment called 'Travel details'.*

Humour

THE GOLD FRAME

The Modern Frame Works was actually an extra-large wooden packing case mounted on wobbly legs tucked in a gap between a drug store and a radio repair shop. Its owner, Datta, with his concave figure, silver-rimmed glasses and a complexion of seasoned timber, fitted into his shop with the harmony of a fixture.

He was a silent, hardworking man. He gave only laconic answers to the questions his customers asked and strongly discouraged casual friends who tried to intrude on his zone of silence with their idle gossip. He was always seen sitting hunched up, surrounded by a confusion of cardboard pieces, bits of wood, glass sheets, boxes of nails, glue bottles, paint tins and other odds and ends that went into putting a picture in a frame. In this medley a glass-cutter or a pencil stub was often lost and that was when he would uncoil from his posture and grope impatiently for it. Many times he had to stand up and shake his dhoti vigorously to dislodge the lost object. This operation rocked the whole shop, setting the pictures on the walls gently swinging.

There was not an inch of space that was not covered by a picture; gods, saints, hockey players, children, cheap prints of the Mona Lisa, national leaders, wedding couples, Urdu calligraphy, the snow-clad Fujiyama and many others co-existed with a cheerful incongruity like some fabulous world awaiting order and arrangement.

A customer standing outside the shop on the pavement, obstructing the stream of jostling pedestrians, announced, 'I want this picture framed.' Datta, with his habitual indifference, ignored him and continued to be engaged in driving screws into the sides of a frame. 'I want a really good job done, no matter how much it costs.' The customer volunteered the information, unwrapping a faded newspaper and exposing a sepia-brown photograph of an old man. It was sharp and highly glazed in spite of its antiquity.

'What sort of a frame would you like?' Datta asked, still bent over his work.

'The best, of course. Do you expect I would stint where this great soul is concerned?'

Datta gave a side glance and caught a glimpse of the photograph; just another elderly person of those days, he told himself; a standard portrait of a grandfather, a philanthropist, a social worker, with the inevitable whiskers and top-heavy cascading turban it could be any one of these. At least half a dozen people came to him every month bearing similar portraits, wanting to demonstrate their homage to the person in the picture in the shape of a glittering frame.

The customer was describing the greatness of the old man; extravagant qualities of nobility, compassion and charity were being generously attributed to him in a voice that came close to the chanting of a holy scripture. '. . . If this world had just a few more like him, believe me, it would certainly have been a different place. Of course, there are demons who may not agree with me. They are out to disgrace his name and destroy his memory. But he is God in my home!'

'What sort of a frame do you want?' Datta interrupted. 'Plain, wooden, lacquer, gold, plastic or just enamel painted?' He waved a casual hand towards the pictures on the wall. The customer silently surveyed the various frames. After some time Datta heard him mumble, 'I want the best . . .'

'I don't have any second-rate stuff in my shop,' Datta said.

He was shown a number of samples; plain, decorative, floral, geometrical, thin, hefty and so forth. The customer was baffled by the variety.

He examined the selection before him for a long time as if he was unsure of his judgement and was afraid of enshrining his saviour for ever in some ugly cheap frame.

Datta came to his rescue and recommended one with a profusion of gold leaves and winding creepers and, in order to clear any lingering doubt he might still harbour in regard to its quality, added: 'It is German! Imported!'

The customer at once seemed impressed and satisfied. Datta next asked, 'You want a plain mount or a cut mount?' and watched the puzzled look return. Again he helped the man out by showing his various mounts and suggested that a cut mount looked more elegant.

'All right, let me have a cut mount then. Is that a cut mount?' he asked, pointing to a framed picture on the wall of a soulful-looking lady in an oval cut mount. 'I like that shape. Will it cost much?'

'No. Frame, mount, glass all will cost seventeen rupees.' The customer had expected it would be more. He pretended to be shocked all the same and tried to bargain. Datta withdrew to his corner without replying and began to cut a piece of plywood. The customer hung about uncertainly for some time and finally asked, 'When will you have it ready?' and barely heard the reply over the vibrating noise of the saw on the plywood, 'Two weeks from today.'

Datta had learnt by long experience that his customers never came punctually. They came days in advance and went away disappointed or came months later, and some never turned up at all and their pictures lay unclaimed in a box, gathering dust and feeding cockroaches and silver fish. Therefore he made frames for those who came to him and visited him at least twice before he actually executed their orders.

Ten days later the tall, rustic-looking man appeared and enquired, 'Has the picture been framed? I was passing by and thought I could collect it if it was ready.' Datta cast a side look at him and continued with his work. 'I know I have come four days early,' the customer grinned nervously. 'Will it be ready by Tuesday?' Datta merely nodded without shifting attention from a tiny nail which he, with precise rhythmic strokes, was driving into a frame, but sensed the man's obsessive attachment to the photograph. He told himself there would be trouble if he did not deliver the order on the promised date.

Next morning he made that his first job, keeping aside all the others.

The photograph was lying on a shelf among many others. He took it and carefully kept it on a wooden plank on the floor. Then he looked for the pencil stub for marking the measurements. As usual it was missing. He swept his hand all round him impatiently, scattering fragments of glass and wood.

False shapes that he mistook for the pencil harassed him no end and stoked his anger. Frustrated in all his attempts to find it, he finally stood up to shake the folds of his dhoti, an ultimate move which generally yielded results. But he shook the folds so violently that he upset a tin containing white enamel paint and it fell right on the sacred photograph of the old man, emptying its thick, slimy contents on it.

Datta stood transfixed and stared at the disaster at his feet as if he had suddenly lost all faculty of movement. He could not bring himself even to avert his eyes from the horror which he seemed to be cruelly forced to view. Then his spectacles clouded with perspiration and helpfully screened his vision.

When at last he fully recovered his senses he set about rescuing the picture in such desperate hurry that he made a worse mess of it. He rubbed the picture so hard with a cloth that he peeled off thin strips of filmy coating from its surface. Before he realised what he had done half the old man's face and nearly all of his turban were gone.

Datta helplessly looked at the venerable elder transformed into thick black specks sticking to the enamel smeared on the rag in his hand.

He sat with both hands clutching his head; every nerve in his head throbbed as if it would tear itself apart if he did not hold it down.

What answer was he going to offer to the customer who had a fanatic devotion to the photograph he had just mutilated beyond recovery?

His imagination ran wild, suggesting nightmarish consequences to his own dear self and to the fragile inflammable shop.

He racked his brain for a long while till sheer exhaustion calmed his agitated nerves and made him accept the situation with a hopeless resignation. Meanwhile the plethora of gods, saints and sages gazed down at him from the walls with a transcendental smile and seemed to offer themselves to him to pray to. With a fervent appeal in his heart he stared at them.

In his state of mind it did not register for quite a while that a particular photograph of a person on the wall had held his attention rather more than it was qualified to do. It was an ordinary portrait of a middle-aged man in a dark suit and striped tie, resting his right arm jauntily on a studio prop made to look like a fluted Roman pillar. Datta was amazed to see that he had a faint likeness to the late lamented old man. The more he gazed at the face the more convincing it appeared to him. But he dismissed the odd resemblance he saw as one of those tricks of a thoroughly fagged-out mind.

All the same, at the back of his mind an idea began to take shape; he saw the possibility of finding an acceptable substitute! He brought down the old wooden box in which he had kept all the photographs unclaimed over the years. As he rummaged in it, panicky cockroaches and spiders scurried helter-skelter all over the floor. Unmindful of them Datta anxiously searched for the brownish photographs of the old man's vintage. Soon there was a pile before him; he was surprised he could pick up so many which qualified to take the old man's place.

But he had to reject a lot of them. In most of the portraits the subjects sported a very conspicuous flower vase next to them, or over-dressed grandchildren sat on their laps and therefore had to be rejected.

Luckily, there was one with which Datta felt he could take a fair risk; the print had yellowed a bit noticeably but he calculated that the total effect when put in a dazzling gold frame would render it safe.

After a couple of hours' concentrated work he sat back and proudly surveyed the old man's double, looking resplendent in his gold frame. He was so pleased with his achievement that he forgot he was taking perhaps one of the greatest risks any frame-maker ever took! He even became bold enough to challenge the customer if his faking was discovered. 'Look, my dear man', he would say, 'I don't know who has been fooling you! That's the picture you brought here for framing. Take it or throw it away!'

The days that followed were filled with suspense and anxiety. Datta feared that the customer would surprise him at an unguarded moment making him bungle the entire, carefully-thought-out plot. But the man turned up promptly a couple of days later. At that moment Datta was bent over a piece of work and slightly stiffened as he heard the voice, shrill with expectation, ask, 'Is it ready?'

Datta's heart began to race and to compose himself he let a whole minute pass without answering. Then he put aside the scissors in his hand with slow deliberation and reached out to take the neatly wrapped package in a corner.

'Ah, it is ready!' the customer exclaimed with childish delight, at the same time mumbling flattering tributes to Datta for his promptness and so on. He spread his arms widely with

dramatic exuberance to receive the photograph as if it was actually a long-lost person he was greeting.

But Datta took his time removing the wrapper from the frame. The customer waited impatiently, filling in the time showering more praises on his worshipful master who was to adorn the wall of his home.

Datta finally revealed the glittering frame and held it towards him.

The customer seemed visibly struck by its grandeur and fell silent like one who had entered the inner sanctum of a temple. Datta held his breath and watched the man's expression. With every second that passed he was losing his nerve and thought that in another moment he would betray the big hoax he had played.

Suddenly he saw the customer straighten, the reverential look and benevolent expression vanished from his face.

'What have you done?' he demanded, indignantly. For Datta the moment seemed familiar for he had already gone through it a thousand times night and day since he splashed the white paint on the original photograph.

Several times he had rehearsed his piece precisely for this occasion.

But before he could open his mouth the customer shouted with tremendous authority in his bearing, 'Now, don't deny it! I clearly remember asking for a cut mount with an oval shape. This is square. Look!'

R.K. Laxman

Comprehension

A. *Read the given text carefully and answer the following questions briefly.*

1. What was the intention of the customer in this story when he went to Datta?
2. What feature of the photograph made Datta think of it as just another photograph of an elderly person of those days?
3. What was the disaster that struck the photograph? What was Datta's reaction to this disaster?
4. How did Datta plan to repair the damage that had occurred?
5. How did Datta go about his plan of action?
6. Explain the humour in the ending of the story.

B. *Choose from a, b and c the correct endings to the following sentences.*

1. The customer examined the selection before him for a long time
   a. as he could not find anything suitable.
   b. as he did not want to make a suitable choice.
   c. as he was unsure of his own judgment with regard to what he should take.

2. Datta had learnt by long experience that
   a. customers never came at the right time when they were requested to come.
   b. customers were very demanding and could not wait.
   c. customers had no sense of taste and he had to advise them on everything.
3. When Datta unwrapped the frame and showed it to the customer
   a. the man was furious.
   b. he was visibly impressed.
   c. he took it quietly.

Vocabulary

Prefixes and suffixes are used to change the meanings of words. For example, the letters 'ion' are used to change words into nouns, 'ise' is used to change nouns into verbs and so on. Prefixes can also be used to convey opposites, for example, 'impatient' is the opposite of 'patient', 'immoral' is the opposite of 'moral' and so on.

activate	⇨	activation
negate	⇨	negation

A. *Give the noun forms of the following with 'ion', 'ism, 'ity', etc.*

procrastinate	reflect	definite	simulate
synchronise	subjective	paternal	united
fraternal	diverse	vivacious	vital
credulous	creative		

B. *Add prefixes to convert the following words to their opposites.*

credible	equal
permissible	penetrable
personal	polite
sincere	soluble
human	hospitable

C. *Look up the following words in a dictionary. Find out how each word is pronounced, which syllable of the word is stressed, the part of speech it belongs to (noun, verb, pronoun, etc.), and in case the word has more than one core meaning, identify the sense in which the word is used in the text that you have just read.*

1. confusion	3. stub
2. extravagant	4. baffled
5. conspicuous	6. vintage

D. *Give one-word substitutes for each group of words below.*

1.	able to be heard	_u_ib__
2.	cause to swell with fluid or gas	__o__
3.	occurring before the proper time	___m__ur_
4.	lacking the quantity or quality required	i__de____e
5.	give added strength to	_e_n___c_
6.	drive out or expel from a position or place	o___

Grammar

The finite verb is the most important word in a sentence. You cannot make a sentence without a finite verb. Whether a sentence is in the positive or negative or interrogative it must have a finite verb.

The finite verb in a sentence can be transitive or it can be *intransitive.*

A *transitive* verb needs a word called an object to complete its meaning.

Finite verbs which are intransitive do not need an object to complete the meaning of the sentence,

e.g. Meera can run.
She sings.
Dogs bark.
They roamed far from home.
We returned (late/in time for dinner).

The underlined words in the sentences below are the objects of the verbs.

The teacher reads out a story every day.
The students completed the experiment.

The finite verbs in the sentences above are transitive and need an object to complete the meaning of the sentences.

Remember that when the main finite verb of a sentence is either the verb 'be' or 'have', it does not take an object. It takes a complement, and cannot be put into the passive form. Remember only sentences with a transitive main verb and an object can be changed into the passive form. Sentences with intransitive verbs cannot be put into the passive form.

A. *Rewrite the following sentences so that they begin with the underlined words.*

1. The war was fought by the foot soldiers.
2. This song used to be sung by my grandmother in the old days when I was young.
3. The tigers were being fed by their keeper when we arrived at the zoo.

4. The play was written by one of the students.
5. To make tea, the water was first brought to the boil by us.
6. The visitors must be greeted with a smile of welcome by them.
7. The bangles were made by our goldsmith.
8. The patients were looked after very well by the nurse.

B. *Rewrite the following sentences so that they begin with the underlined words. Drop phrases that begin with 'by' if followed by a pronoun.*

1. Everyone greatly admired the new dress.
2. You must do this work very carefully.
3. We will take care of all the details.
4. We will fly the flag half mast on Gandhiji's death anniversary.
5. They grow cotton in many parts of the country.
6. The doctor will examine you tomorrow.
7. They spoke a great deal on the topic.
8. Lightning rent the sky and strong winds tore down the trees in the mountainside.

C. *Read the passage below. A word has been omitted in each line. Mark the omissions with a ^ and write the omitted word in the space provided. The first omitted word has been inserted as an example.*

He moved ^ the undergrowth silently, crouching and crawling	through
his stomach and every now and then raising his head to	(1) ______
see far he was from the track. A large uprooted tree lay between him	(2) ______
and the open track, and if he only get behind the tree, he could	(3) ______
keep a longish stretch of the road observation. The only	(4) ______
snag getting behind the fallen tree would be that it would then	(5) ______
be impossible to get away there without being seen. In the grey-green	(6) ______
darkness the jungle dawn it was easy enough to approach the tree	(7) ______
unseen, but once there was almost certain that he would have to wait	(8) ______
until evening to get away.	

Listening

Listen to the sentences that your teacher will play for you on the tape. For each sentence, indicate the correct placement of stress by choosing one of the items in the pairs given below.

1. 'permit per'mit	4. 'desert de'sert
2. 'object ob'ject	5. 'present pre'sent
3. 'survey sur'vey	6. 'perfect per'fect

Speaking

Listen to the dialogues that your teacher will play for you on tape and also read their transcripts in your book. Pay attention to the italicised expressions in the transcripts. The dialogues present situations where an apology is called for.

Dialogue 1 (formal)

(Asif Abdullah supplies material for a construction company. There is a delay in the delivery of a truckload of steel because of which the company had to lose three valuable days of work besides wages paid to the workers. Asif apologises to the managing director of the company.)

Asif: Ms Bharadwaj, *I must apologise for* the delay in the delivery of the steel you had ordered. *I fully understand* the loss it must have meant to you in terms of both time and money. *It all happened because of* the transport strike across the state and I was really helpless in the matter. *I'm sincerely sorry and hope you'll excuse the delay and give me another chance* to do business with your company.

Ms Bharadwaj: Mr Abdullah, you're right about the loss that the delay on your part caused us. *We don't blame you fully* for we do know that it was caused by the strike. We think, though, that you could have made some other arrangement to let us have the material on time. However, *we'll accept your apologies and hope that this kind of a thing does not happen again.*

Asif: Thank you for being so understanding, Ms Bharadwaj.

Dialogue 2 (informal)

(Jeevan knocks over a crystal vase, breaking it into pieces. His mother scolds him, and he apologises to her.)

Mother: Jeevan, you've broken my favourite vase! How can you be so careless!

Jeevan: Ma, *I'm so sorry.* I was running to answer the telephone and slipped on the freshly mopped floor. *Please forgive me.*

Mother: *All right, but do be a little careful in future* when you go about the house.

Jeevan: Thanks, Ma! I promise that I won't run about inside the house again.

Exercise A

You will now hear on tape some expressions used in both formal and informal situations to make apologies and also to respond to them. Listen to each item and repeat it, using the right intonation.

- I must apologise for.....
- I'm terribly sorry about......
- Please accept my sincere apologies.
- I hope you'll excuse me.
- Please forgive me.
- I'm so sorry.
- It won't happen again, I promise.
- I'm really ashamed of myself.
- It's quite all right.
- I really hope it won't happen again.
- No need to feel so bad about it. These things happen.

Exercise B

Working in pairs, write and enact the following situations in the form of brief dialogues choosing appropriate expressions from those given above.

1. Parveen forgets to wish her friend Anju on her birthday and calls her to apologise. Anju assures her that it is all right.
2. Ashok Garg apologises to his senior colleague, Tony Alfred, for a mistake that he made in drafting a legal document. Alfred excuses Ashok.

Writing

Note making

Some useful points to remember

- Making notes from a lecture or talk or from an article or book is a very useful study skill.
- Besides helping you remember what you heard or read sometime ago, making notes will enable you to organise your own thoughts better. This is because while making notes, you will also be considering the importance of the different points in the matter you are listening or reading to and drawing your own conclusions about them.
- When you make notes, you must take down the important points. You can do this by picking up signals received from the speaker's tone or by looking for special words that introduce new information.

- Important points that you identify can be written down briefly in the form of words and phrases and as meaningful abbreviations.
- You can either use standard abbreviations (such as 'e.g.' and 'etc.') or create your own (as in 'engg.' and 'tech.').
- Words such as articles and pronouns can be dropped unless they are necessary in order to understand the notes.
- You can also use diagrams and tables in your notes to summarise information.

You can follow the steps below to make notes from an essay or an article or a chapter from a book.

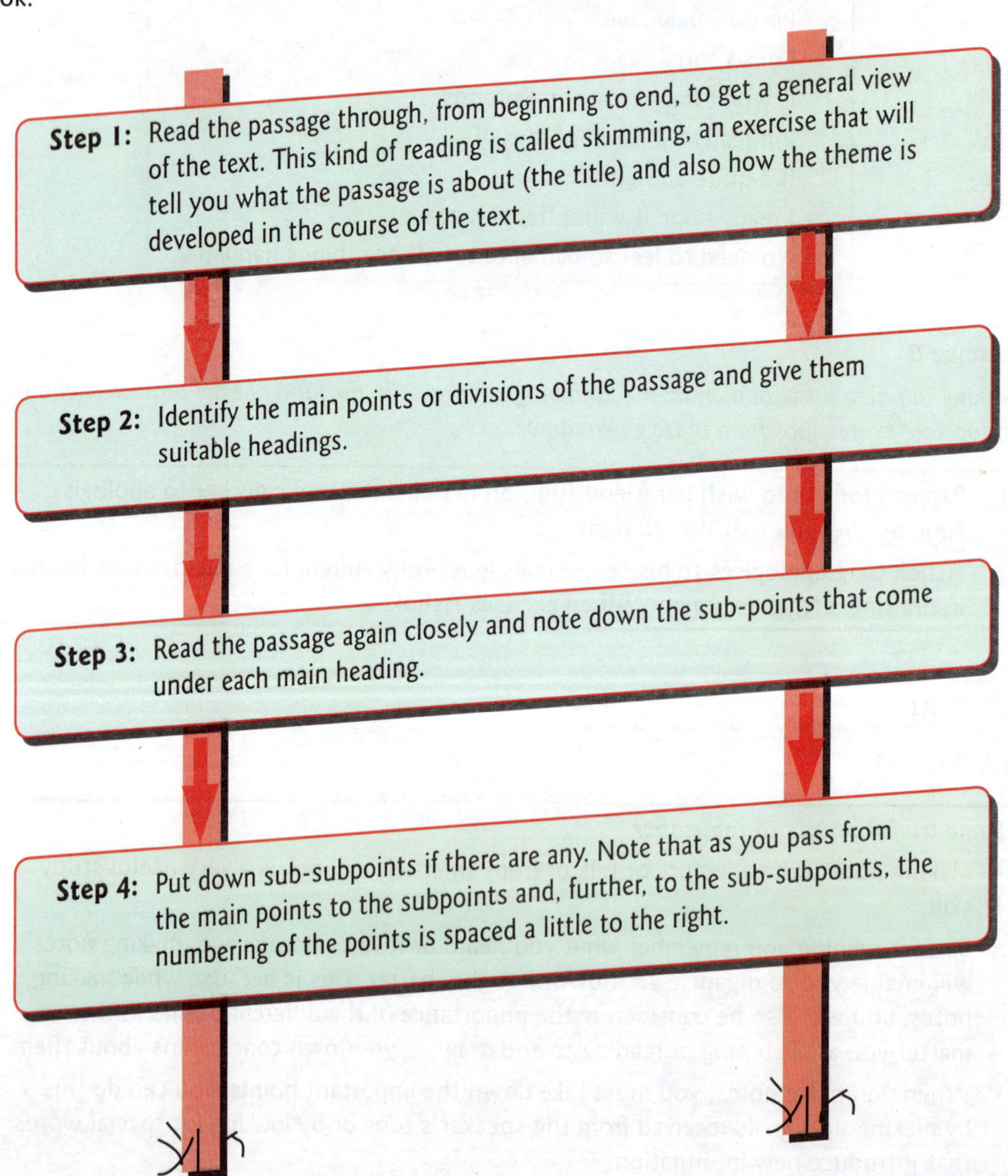

Look at the following framework that you can use to make notes and note the numbering of the main headings, the subheadings and further divisions.

A. ....

1. ....

a. ....

b. ....

i. ....

ii. ....

2. ....

a. ....

i. ....

ii. ....

b. ....

B. ....

Another system of notation, known as the decimal notation, uses only the arabic numerals, as shown below.

1. ....

1.1 ....

1.2 ....

1.2.1 ....

1.2.2 ....

1.3 ....

A short passage and a specimen set of notes are given below for your reference.

There are several kinds of crossword puzzles. The first is the prize competition type in which the person who finds the correct answers gets a big prize. But the answers are very hard to find, since several words appear equally appropriate: 'bad', 'mad' or 'sad', for example, in the clue sentence, '– – – people are seldom popular'. Such competitions attract people who are fond of gambling, because by paying a small entry fee, they can win big prizes.
The second type of crossword puzzle is one in which there is only one possible answer to every clue. But this answer is elusive and calls for some detective work on our part. The clue gives only hints about the word. A clue like 'mate changes to flesh for food' will elude you till you realise that by changing the spelling of 'mate' you get 'meat'. Your comprehension and your general knowledge are put to the test. The effort to solve such crosswords is an

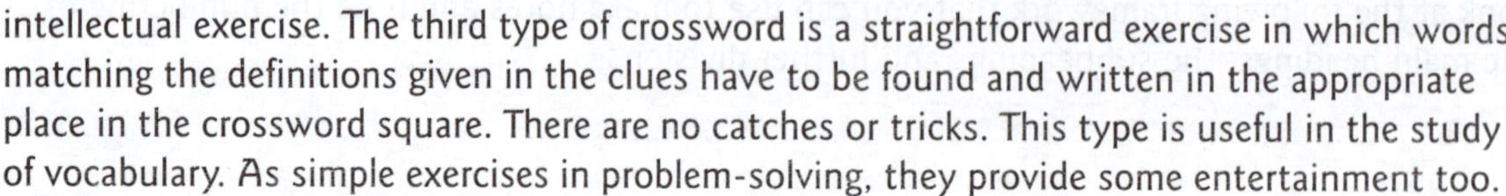

intellectual exercise. The third type of crossword is a straightforward exercise in which words matching the definitions given in the clues have to be found and written in the appropriate place in the crossword square. There are no catches or tricks. This type is useful in the study of vocabulary. As simple exercises in problem-solving, they provide some entertainment too.

Exercises

A. *Read the given passage, suggest a suitable title for it and make notes following the steps outlined above.*

Acupuncture, a system of treatment of diseases, has been practised in China for nearly five thousand years. It consists in the rapid insertion of fine steel needles, about six centimetres long, in particular spots on the body of the patient. After inserting the needle, the doctor twirls it between his thumb and forefinger. There are hundreds of acupuncture points on the body. When a puncture is made on a spot on the body, energy flows from there along lines known as 'meridians' to the diseased organs. This flow of energy helps to restore the balance of the system and thus correct the disorder. The points of treatment may be far from the seat of the disease. For example, to cure a toothache, the acupuncturist may insert a needle on the palm of the patient.

Although China is considered to be the country where acupuncture originated, some forms of treatment resembling it have been reported from other parts of the world by anthropologists. Among some ancient tribes, stones and arrows were used to prick the skin. In another form of treatment, the skin on particular spots of the body was burnt to effect a cure for certain diseases. Whether these kinds of treatment can rightly be classed with acupuncture can be known only after further research.

For long acupuncture was dismissed by the West as a form of superstition like witchcraft and magic cure. Even in China, admiration for the western system of medicine was so great that the native systems of treatment were neglected or mistrusted. Moreover, the theoretical basis for acupuncture that was propounded in China was a mixture of spirituality, philosophy and physiology. This stood in the way of its acceptance by Chinese scientists.

During the 1960s acupuncture came to the notice of western scientists, who viewed it with scepticism as well as curiosity. Doctors from Europe went to China to make a first-hand study of this strange form of treatment. What they saw convinced them that acupuncture worked. Not only were diseases cured, but even operations were performed after administering anaesthesia by acupuncture. The patient in such an operation could see and know what was being done but felt no pain. After the operation he could get up and walk away. Doctors in other parts of the world took acupuncture seriously and some of them trained themselves and set up practice in their countries. In China itself, the status of acupuncture rose when Chairman Mao officially ranked acupuncturists with other physicians.

B. *Listen to a speech or lecture of three to five minutes' duration. It could be your principal's address at the morning assembly or a part of your teacher's lecture or a short talk on television. Jot down points and arrange them in the form of notes.*

C. *Read the passage given below. Then make notes from it. You will be using the notes in a writing exercise in unit 9.*

Fibres are thin long pieces of material which are spun into threads for making cloth, ropes, etc. They are strong along their length and are also flexible. That is, they have a good amount of tensile strength. Fibres can broadly be classified into two categories: fibres of natural origin and fibres of artificial origin. Artificial fibres can again be subdivided into two groups: modified forms of natural fibres and synthetic fibres which are directly synthesised.

Fibres of natural origin are further classified into two groups: those of vegetable origin and those of animal origin. The vegetable origin fibres are cotton, jute, hemp and flax. Amongst the animal fibres, wool from sheep and from a breed of goats found in Kashmir is the most common. There is also another type of fibre produced by the moth. These are also of animal origin. Besides these, there is another natural source of fibre, the asbestos fibre. Asbestos is a natural silicate fibre found in rocks. These mineral fibres are used in equipment requiring insulation and in fireproof screens or fire dresses in the form of sheets of spun threads.

The natural fibres of vegetable origin are mostly cellulose whereas the animal fibres are protein compounds and contain sulphur. Thus whenever an animal fibre is burnt it gives a bad smell of burnt sulphur.

Most of the fibres now in use are human-made fibres or natural fibres modified by humans. The mercerised cotton fibre for example, is natural cotton fibre treated in such a way that the flat fibres become round and get a glaze. It then looks like silk and is used for clothes, etc. Also, the cellulose from fibres is taken and treated to make entirely new fibres. The artificial fibres thus made are also cellulose fibres but of an entirely new structure. The cellulose is digested in an alkaline medium and the resultant orange mass is passed through small orifices in an acid bath where it again forms into cellulose fibres. The process is known as the viscose process and the fibre formed is called viscose rayon. In another method, cellulose is turned into cellulose acetate which is dissolved in acetone and the solution forced out through orifices into the air where it dries into fibres. These fibres, though inflammable, are finer than viscose rayon and is termed acetate rayon.

Besides the artificially made cellulose fibres, there are fibres entirely synthesised by us. The most common amongst them is nylon. This is a polymer formed by the reaction of hexamethylene diamine and adepic acid. The polymer is of condensation type and is barely inflammable. When spun into threads and ropes, it is very strong and does not absorb water. It was formerly named 'Polymer 6', and during the war it came to be called 'Nylon' (an amalgamation of New York and London).

The other important polymer fibre synthetically made is terylene. This was synthesised by ICI. and has the composition glycol terephthalate. This polymer, though inflammable, is crease resistant and so is generally used for suit making. The same polyester was

synthesised in the USA. under the name Dacron. Besides these, there are other polymer fibres such as Orlon which substitute wool. The synthetic glass-fibres are also important.

Fibres are intensively used for commercial purposes. Nylon is used in place of steel ropes in parachutes and balloons. Glass fibres are used in high-brightness television receivers, in cathode-ray tubes, in optical equipment and in buildings. Synthetic fibres are now generally appreciated by the modern world for their utility in clothing, packaging, etc. They have numerous advantages over cotton, silk and wool.

(This is an abridged version of Sri Subir Kumar Mitra's essay, which was adjudged the best in 1966 in the Jagadis Bose National Science Talent Search.)

Language games

Get into small groups to play this game. Expand each sentence at the centre of the flowers below in different ways, using the hints given in the petals round it. The group that makes the longest meaningful sentence wins.

1\.
Yasmin went to school.
Yasmin who?
when?
manner?
who else?
which school?
purpose?
cause?
mode of travel?

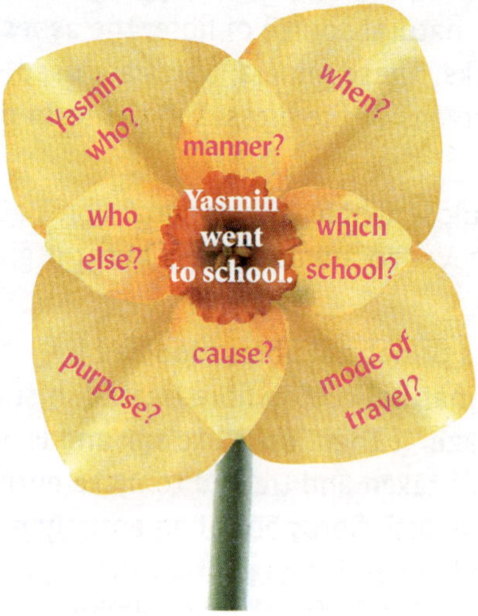

2\.
It rained.
when?
how?
where?
duration?
effect?
cause?
speaker's attitude?

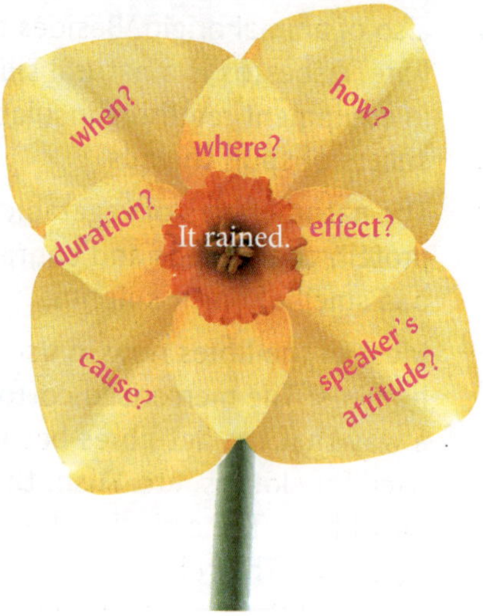

3\.
Vikram met Joseph.
Vikram who?
occasion?
Joseph who?
time?
day?
purpose?
place?

Health and Medicine

SAVE YOUR LIVER

Weighing at three to four pounds, about one fiftieth of the total body heft, the liver is the largest of the glands. It is divided into two great lobes, the right and left, and two small lobes, the caudate and the quadrate. In the strangely beautiful dynamism of embryology, the liver appears as a tree that grows out of the virgin land of the foregut in order to increase its metabolic and digestive function. Its spreading crown of tissue continues to draw nourishment from the blood vessels of the intestine. Legion are the functions of this workhorse, the most obvious of which is the manufacture and secretion of a pint of bile a day, without which golden liquor we could not digest so much as a single raisin; and therefore, contrary to the legend that the liver is an organ given to man for him to be bilious with, in its absence we should become rather more cantankerous and grouchy than we are. This is enough reason for us to guard it against all its enemies, the deadliest of which is alcohol.

Man's romance with alcohol had its origins in the Neolithic Age or earlier, presumably from the accidental tasting by some curious fellow of, let's say, fermented honey, or mead as it is written in *Beowulf*. The attainment of the resultant euphoria has remained a continuous striving of the human race with the exception of the perverse era of Prohibition, which presumed to tear asunder that which Nature had joined in absolute harmony. From its first appearance on the planet, alcohol has never been absent from the scene.

The human body is perfectly suited for the ingestion of alcohol, and for its rapid utilisation. In that sense we are not unlike alcohol lamps. Endless is our eagerness to devour alcohol. Witness the facts that it is absorbed not only from the intestine, as are all other foods, but directly from the stomach as well. It can be taken in by the lungs as an inhalant, and even by the rectum if given as an enema. Once incorporated into the body, it is to the liver that belongs the task of oxidising the alcohol. But even the sturdiest liver can handle only a drop or two at a time, and the remainder swirls ceaselessly about in the bloodstream, is exhaled by the lungs and thus provides the police with a sure method of detecting and measuring the presence and amount of alcohol ingested. Along the way it bathes the brain with happiness, lifting the inhibitory cortex off the primal swamp of the id and permitting to surface all sorts of delicious urges such as the one to walk into people's houses wearing your wife's hat. Happily enough, the brain is not organically altered by alcohol unless taken in near-lethal amounts. The brain cells are not destroyed by it in any kind of moderate drinking, and if the alcohol is withdrawn from the diet, the brain rapidly awakens and resumes its function at the usual, if not normal, level. One must reckon, nevertheless, with the hangover, which retributive phenomenon is devised to make the drinker feel guilty.

It was a French physician who first described the disease known as cirrhosis of the liver, near the turn of the nineteenth century. His name, René Théophile Hyacinthe Laënnec. This fastidious gentleman was the very same whose aversion to applying his naked ear to the perfumed but unbathed bosoms of his patients inspired him to invent the stethoscope, which idea he plagiarised from a group of street urchins playing with rolled-up paper. The entire medical world continues to pay homage to Laënnec for his gift of space interpersonal. As if this were not enough, he permitted himself to be struck by the frequent appearance at autopsy of livers that were yellow, knobby and hard. This marvel he named cirrhosis, from the Greek word for tawny, *kirrhos*. The liver appears yellow because it is fatty, hard because it is scarred, and knobby because the regeneration of liver tissue between the scars produces little mounds or hillocks. It was suspected by Laënnec, and is known by all the rest of us today, that by far the most common cause of cirrhosis is the consumption of alcohol.

Alcohol is metabolised in the liver by a fiercely efficient enzyme called alcohol dehydrogenase, and transformed directly into energy, which would all be terribly nice were it not for the unjust fact that alcohol is poisonous to the liver, causing it to become loaded with fat. If enough is imbibed, and enough fat is deposited in the liver, this organ takes on the yellowish colour noted by Laënnec. Still more booze, and the liver becomes heavy with fat, swelling so that it emerges from beneath the protective rib cage and bulges down into the vulnerable soft white underbelly. There it can be palpated by the examining fingers, and even seen protruding on the right side of the abdomen in some cases.

Even today, the progression from this fatty stage to the frank inflammation and scarring that are the hallmarks of cirrhosis is not well understood. Factors other than continued drinking pertain here. One of these is susceptibility. Jews, for instance, are not susceptible. One sees precious few cirrhotic Jews. It was formerly averred by somewhat chauvinistic Jewish hepatologists that Jews didn't get cirrhosis because they didn't drink much, what with their strong, dependable family ties, and their high motivation, and their absolute need to excel in order to survive. They didn't need to drink. But Jews are now among the most emancipated of drinkers and, with all the fervour of new converts, are causing such virtuosi as the Irish and the French to glance nervously over their shoulders. Still, the Jews do not get cirrhosis. This is not to say that they are not alcoholics. It has been reported by more than one visiting professor of medicine that noticeable

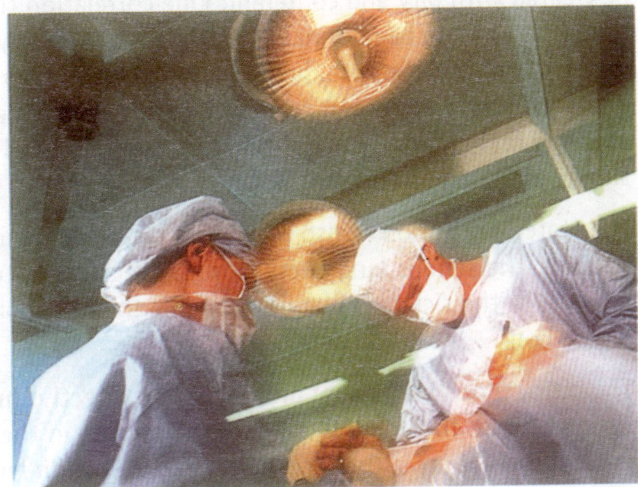

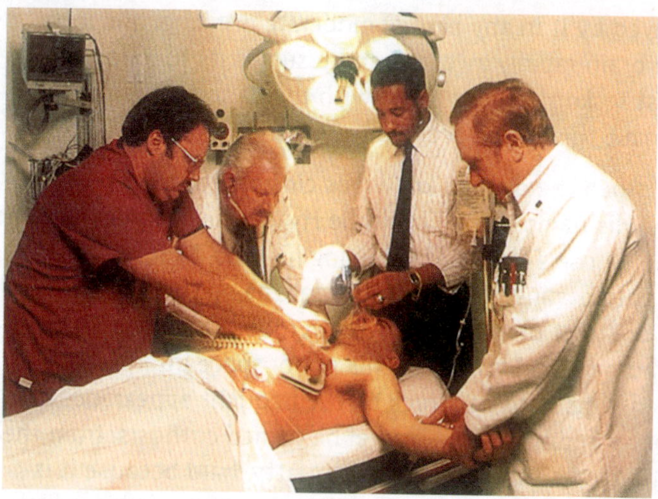

segments of the population of Israel get and stay drunk for quite heroic periods of time. It is also reported that their livers remain enviably healthy.

Another measure of susceptibility is, brace yourselves, the absence of hair on the chest. In males, of course. Unpelted men of the sort idealised by bathing-suit and underwear manufacturers are sitting ducks for the onset of cirrhosis. All other things being equal, women, the marrying kind, would do well to turn aside from such vast expanses of naked chest skin and to cultivate a taste for the simian. It was formerly thought that cirrhotic men lost their chest hair. Not so. They never had any to begin with.

Lastly, it is said by some that climate is a factor: the closer to the equator, the more vulnerable the liver. Thus, a quantity of alcohol that scarcely ruffles the frozen current of a Norwegian's blood would scatter madness and fever into the brain of an Indian.

There is a difference, I hasten to add, between imbibers of alcohol and alcoholics. Both develop fatty livers, true, but no one has shown conclusively that a fatty liver is the precursor of cirrhosis. One martini increases the fat content of the liver sufficiently so that it can be seen by the use of special stains under the microscope. In other words, a single martini increases the fat in a liver by one half per cent of the weight of the organ, above a normal three per cent. In the alcoholic this commonly reaches a death-defying twenty-five per cent. But you don't have to be an alcoholic to get cirrhosis. Some quite modest drinkers get it. Nor does it matter the purity of the spirits consumed. Beer, wine, and whiskey equally offend, and he who would take comfort from the idea that he drinks only beer, or only wine, is to be treated with pity and contempt. One correlation that does hold water is the duration of time that one has been drinking. Cirrhosis is primarily a disease of the forties or fifties. Even here we cannot generalise, however, for great numbers of younger people are afflicted, and one patient within my ken was an eighteen-year-old girl whose voluminous liver could be felt abutting on her groin just eight months after she had retired to her room with a continuous supply of Thunderbird wine.

The state of nutrition is also a factor in the development of cirrhosis. It is no secret that boozers, the serious kind, stop eating, especially protein, either because they can't afford it or because the sick liver just can't handle the metabolism of protein well, and the appetite is warned off.

The nitrogenous material of protein passes directly through the diseased liver and exerts a toxic effect on the brain. If one restricts protein in the diet of cirrhotics, the brain improves. A case in point is Sir Andrew Aguecheek of *Twelfth Night,* whose eccentricity, emotional

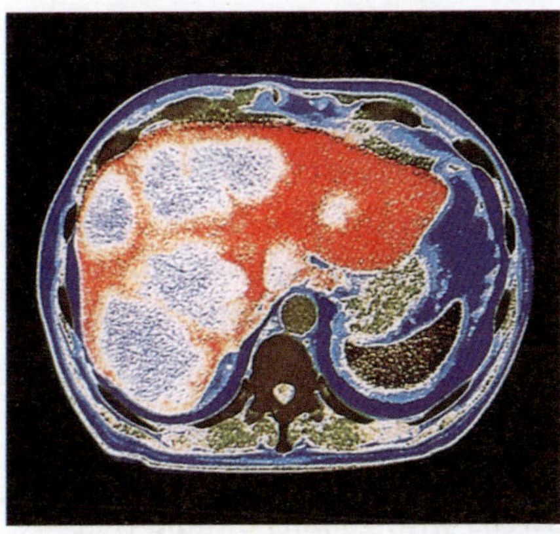

lability and restricted vocabulary were almost certainly due to the organic brain syndrome of liver disease due to intolerance of nitrogen.

In an analysis of the inhabitants of Chicago's Skid Row, it was observed that a customary diet consisted of alcohol in any form and jelly doughnuts. Yet in the cases of thirty-nine hundred such folk whose death certificates were signed out as cirrhosis, only ten per cent were actually found to have the disease at autopsy. Thus it might be stated that alcoholics exceed cirrhotics by nine to one—or that only ten per cent of alcoholics get cirrhosis.

What is clearly needed is a test to find out which are the ten per cent that are going to get it, so that the rest of us can enjoy ourselves. At the moment I prefer to take comfort from the example of such valiant topers as Winston Churchill, who swallowed a fifth of whiskey a day all the while leading Great Britain in her finest hour, and went on to die in his nineties, still holding his fingers up like that. It is also true that if one, moved by some transcendental vision or goaded by ill-conceived guilt, abstains from further drinking, in short order all the excess fat departs from the liver and it once again regains its pristine colour and size. In this way do spree drinkers inadvertently rest their livers and avoid the cirrhosis we slow but steadies risk. Thus something can be said for periodic abstinence, a wisdom one would hesitate to translate into other vices.

Envision, if you will, a house whose stones are living hexagonal tiles not unlike those forming the bathroom floors of first-class hotels. These are the hepatocytes, the cellular units of the liver. Under the microscope they have a singular uniformity, each as like unto its fellow as the antlers of a buck, and all fitted together with a lovely imprecision so as to form a maze of crooked hallways and oblong rooms. Coursing through this muralium of tissue are two arborisations of blood vessels, the one bringing food and toxins from the intestine, the other delivering oxygen from the heart and lungs. Winding in and among these networks is a system of canaliculi that puts to shame all the aqueductal glories of Greece and Rome. Through these sluice the rivers of bile, gathering strength and volume as the little ducts at the periphery meet others, going into ones of larger calibre, which in turn fuse, and so on until there are two large tubes emerging from the undersurface of the liver. Within this magic house are all the functions of the liver carried out. The food we eat is picked over, sorted out, and stored for future use in the cubicles of the granary. Starch is converted to glycogen, which is released in the form of energy as the need arises. Protein is broken down into its building blocks, the amino acids, later to be fashioned into more YOU, as old tissues die off and need to be replaced. Fats are stored until sent forth to provide warmth and comfort. Vitamins and antibodies are released into the bloodstream. Busy is the word for the liver. Deleterious substances ingested, inadvertently like DDT or intentionally like alcohol, are either changed into harmless components and excreted into the intestine, or stored in locked closets to be kept isolated from the rest of the body. Even old blood cells are pulverized and recycled.

But there are limits. Along comes that thousandth literary lunch and—Pow! the dreaded wrecking ball of cirrhosis is unslung. The roofs and walls of the hallways, complaining under their burden of excess fat, groan and buckle. Inflammation sets in, and whole roomfuls of liver cells implode and die, and in their place comes the scarring that twists and distorts the channels, pulling them into impossible angulation. Avalanches block the flow of bile and heavy tangles of fibre impede the absorption and secretion. This happens not just in one spot but all over, until the gigantic architecture is a mass of sores and wounds, the old ones scarring over as new ones break down.

The obstructed bile, no longer able to flow down to the gut, backs up into the bloodstream to light up the skin and eyes with the sickly lamp of jaundice. The stool turns toothpaste white in commiseration, the urine dark as wine. The belly swells with gallons of fluid that weep from the surface of the liver, no less than the tears of a loyal servant so capriciously victimized. The carnage spreads. The entire body is discommoded. The blood fails to clot, the palms of the hands turn mysteriously red, and spidery blood vessels leap and crawl on the skin of the face and neck. Male breasts enlarge, and the testicles turn soft and atrophy.

Scared? Better have a drink. You look a little pale. In any case there is no need to be all that glum. Especially if you know something that I know. Remember Prometheus? That poor devil who was chained to a rock, and had his liver pecked out each day by a vulture? Well, he was a classical example of the regeneration of tissue, for every night his liver grew back to be ready for the dreaded diurnal feast. And so will yours grow back, regenerate, reappear, regain all of its old efficiency and know-how. All it requires is quitting the booze, now and then. The ever-grateful, forgiving liver will respond joyously with a multitude of mitoses and cell divisions that will replace the sick tissues with spanking new nodules and lobules of functioning cells. This rejuvenation is carried on with the speed and alacrity of a starfish growing a new ray from the stump of the old. New channels are opened up, old ones dredged out, walls are straightened and roofs shored up. Soon the big house is humming with activity, and all those terrible things I told you happen go away.

And here's something to tuck away and think about whenever you want to feel good. Sixty per cent of all cirrhotics who stop drinking will be alive and well five years later. How unlike the lofty brain which has no power of regeneration at all. Once a brain cell dies, you are forever one shy.

Good old liver!

[Adapted from Richard Selzer, *Best Science Writings: Reading and Insights*]

Comprehension

A. *Read the given text carefully and answer the following questions briefly.*

1. What is one of the most important functions of the liver?
2. How did man's romance with alcohol begin?
3. What are the after-effects of consuming alcohol?
4. What is the most common cause of cirrhosis and what does a cirrhotic liver look like?
5. What are the links between the state of the liver and the kind of nutrition that one has?

B. *Choose from a, b, c and d the correct endings to the following sentences.*

1. The liver can oxidise only a very small quantity of alcohol at a time. The remainder
   a. is vomited.
   b. is exhaled.
   c. is ingested.
   d. is converted into sugar.
2. The intake of alcohol causes the liver to
   a. bleed.
   b. shrink.
   c. become loaded with fat.
   d. regenerate.
3. Alcohol is
   a. absorbed easily only from the intestines.
   b. absorbed easily not only from the intestines but also from the stomach.
   c. not absorbed from the digestive system but taken into the blood directly.
   d. reaches the brain directly when it is ingested.
4. Jews do not get cirrhosis easily
   a. because they do not drink at all.
   b. there is a level of susceptibility which Jews do not touch.
   c. because of their strong family ties.
   d. because they did not know anything about alcohol.

Vocabulary

Give the noun forms of the following adjectives.

scrupulous	permanent	playful	enjoyable
affectionate	dirty	doubtful	hostile
apologetic	sympathetic	equal	accidental
complacent	flexible	fluent	elegant
introductory	solitary	intense	humble

Grammar

Read the sentences below and identify the tenses of the underlined verbs (past continuous, simple past, past perfect or present perfect).

I was suffering from a temporary loss of memory. It was during those difficult days that Sara looked after me as a mother would. She insisted on taking me for a holiday to a seaside resort where she had taken a cottage on rent.

Before we set out she came over to see that everything was in order. 'Are you ready then?' she asked me. 'Have you had some breakfast?' 'Yes, I have,' I answered. ' I have had breakfast.'

'What did you eat?'

'I ate some chapatis and vegetables, I think.'

'Good,' she said. 'And have you packed all you need? Have you taken an extra pair of shoes?' I assured her I had. I had packed all I needed and had remembered the shoes.

'Have you shut all the windows?'

'Yes, I have,' I told her.

'And have you turned off the gas?'

I had not, and I told her I hadn't. So I went in now and turned off the gas. I had remembered to switch off the fans and lights but had forgotten the geyser. So now I switched off the geyser. If I hadn't done that there would have been an explosion. I had forgotten to talk to the neighbours about feeding the cat and dog. If Sara had not taken charge of all these details my pets would have died and that would have ruined my holiday.

Listening

A. *Listen to a dialogue between Seema and Mr Gujral and fill in the blanks in the sentences below.*

1. Seema went on a holiday to .... in the month of ....
2. She went with her .... and ....
3. The weather was .... during most of Seema's holiday.
4. Seema and her mother .... and .... on the days when there were light showers.
5. Other places she saw were ....
6. Two beautiful products that the shops had to offer were ....
7. Nitin spent as much time as he could .... and Papa loved ....
8. Seema brought back from her holiday a .... for Mr Gujral.

B. *Look at the map showing a part of a city on page 75 and follow the directions you will hear on tape to find yourself in front of a building that you have to identify.*

Speaking

Listen to the dialogues that your teacher will play for you on tape and also read their transcripts in your book. Pay attention to the italicised expressions in the transcripts. The dialogues present situations where an invitation is extended and accepted or declined.

Dialogue 1 (formal)

(Mr Gopal Reddy invites two colleagues to his son's engagement dinner.)

Reddy: Good morning, Rita! Good morning, Mrs Iyer! *There's some happy news I must tell you about.*

Rita: *We're so happy for you, Mr Reddy.*

Mrs Iyer: Do tell us what it is, Mr Reddy.

Reddy: *My son, Rahul, is getting engaged on the twenty-fifth of this month. My wife and I will be happy if you both along with your families could come to the engagement that will be followed by a dinner at the YWCA convention centre at seven in the evening.*

Rita: *Congratulations, Mr Reddy, and thanks for the invitation. I'll certainly be there with my family.*

Reddy: *Thank you very much, Rita. We look forward to seeing you.*

Mrs Iyer: *Congratulations, Mr Reddy. Thank you for inviting us. I wish we could have come, but I'm sorry we'll have to miss the engagement.* My brother-in-law is getting married on the same evening. I'm leaving on the twenty-second for Bangalore with my family. *What a pity!*

Reddy: *Yes, it's so disappointing that you won't be able to attend the function. We'll all miss you. However, please don't worry, Mrs Iyer. I understand.*

Dialogue 2 (informal)

(Rema sees her friends Usha and Teja in the colony park and goes up to speak to them.)

Rema: Hello, Usha! Hi, Teja!

Usha and Teja (together): Hi, Rema!

Rema: I was planning to call and speak to you both. *I'm having a small party on Friday evening at five o'clock. Why don't you both come?*

Usha: *Sure, I'd love to!* I'll be there early to help you put finishing touches to everything.

Rema: *Thanks, Usha. It'll be nice having you at the party.*

Teja: The party's on Friday, isn't it? *I'm sorry but I don't think I'll be able to make it.* You see, my mother is getting operated for gall bladder stones on Thursday. I'll need to be with her in the hospital. *Thanks for asking me.*

Rema: *You're welcome, Teja. Everyone's going to miss your music at the party. But we'll make it up some other time.*

Exercise A

You will now hear on tape some expressions used in both formal and informal situations to extend invitations and also to accept and decline them. Listen to each item and repeat it, using the right intonation.

- There's some good news.
- I'm so happy to hear that.
- My son is getting engaged.
- I'll be happy if you and your family could come.
- Are you free tomorrow evening?
- Why don't you join us at a get-together?
- Thank you for the invitation. We'll certainly come.
- It'll be a pleasure.
- Oh, sure. I'd love to come!
- Thank you for inviting me. I wish I could have come.
- I'm afraid I'll not be able to come.
- I'm sorry, but I'll have to miss the engagement.
- What a pity you won't be able to come!
- Thank you so much. We look forward to seeing you.
- Thanks for saying yes. Be there on time.
- It's disappointing that you won't be there.
- We'll all miss you.
- It can't be helped, I suppose. But we'll make it up some other time.

Exercise B

Working in groups of three, write and enact the following situations in the form of brief dialogues choosing appropriate expressions from those given above.

1. The general manager of a company invites two colleagues to lunch. One accepts and the other declines the invitation because of some other engagement.
2. Anita invites her friends, Hari and Rina, to go with her family on a picnic. Rina accepts the invitation but Hari declines it because of urgent work that he has to attend to on that day.

Writing

Precis writing and abstracting

Some useful points to remember

- The precis and the abstract are both summaries that contain all the important points in an essay, article or chapter from a book.
- The function of both is to give an overview of the original and not to support or criticise.

- A precis should be approximately a third of the length of the original while an abstract is even more condensed at ten per cent of the length of the original.
- The difference in the length of the two types of summaries reflects the different reasons for which they are used. You read an abstract of a text to discover if the original will be relevant or useful to you. On the contrary, you read a precis because you are interested in the original but have no time to read it completely.
- The two forms of summarising are of equal importance to the reader, who benefits from having condensed versions of lengthy texts, and to its writer, for whom it is an exercise in reading and understanding the text thoroughly.
- Writing a precis or an abstract is an extension of the activity of note making.
- Precis and abstracting should be done in your words, but keep the key words of the original because these make it possible for a reader to access the summary through a computer search.
- Make use of linking devices to give your summaries the quality of coherence.
- In writing a precis or an abstract, follow the order of ideas as they occur in the original as far as possible.
- The precis and the summary should keep the tone of the original and indicate the writer's attitude towards the subject.
- Illustrations and tables in the original passage can be omitted. Examples can also be left out, but if you think that they would help the reader understand a point better, you can select one or two typical ones for the summary.
- Quotations and similes can either be omitted or changed into simple statements.
- The language of a precis or an abstract must be simple, concise and direct.
- Long phrases can be replaced by single words (e.g. 'organic' for 'plant or animal origin').
- Sentences can be made compact by changing their structure (e.g. 'He confessed his guilt' for 'He confessed that he was guilty of the crime'.)

The steps below will help you in writing a precis or an abstract.

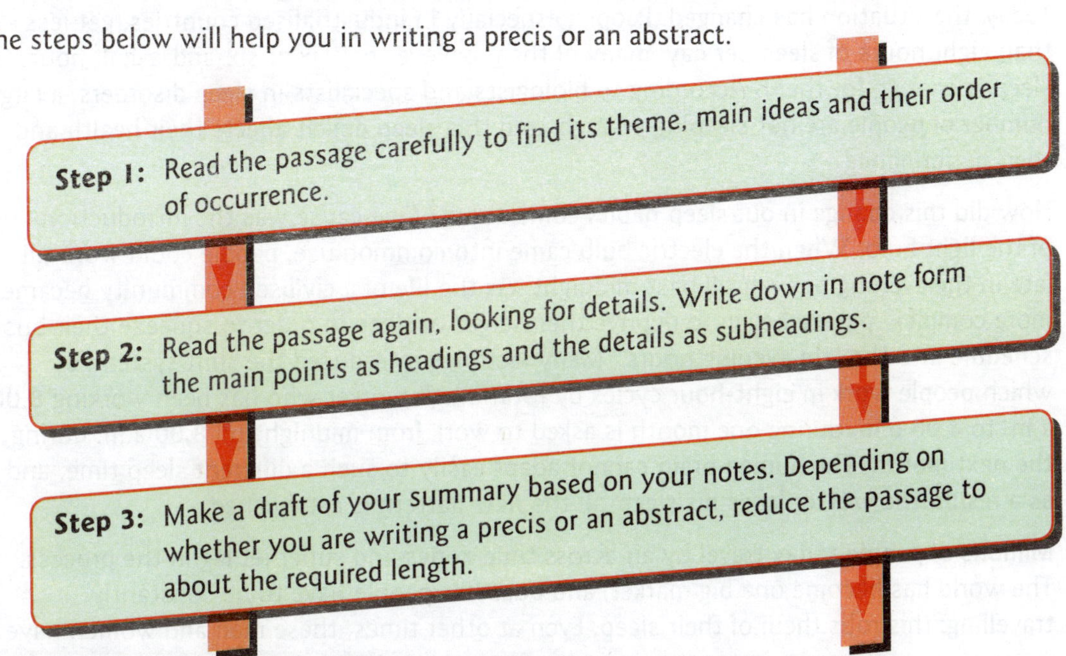

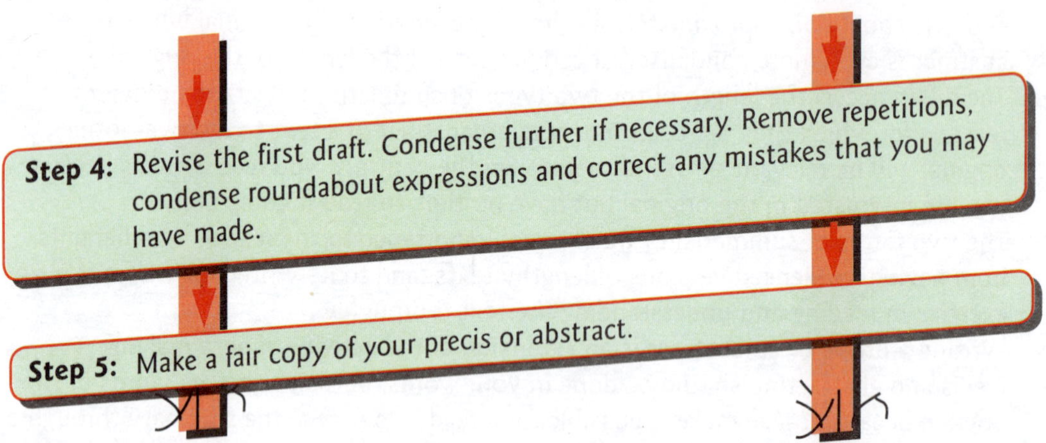

Exercises

A. *Read the passage below. Make notes on it and use these to write the first draft of a precis. Revise your draft to arrive at a final draft of the precis.*

A newborn baby appears to be sleeping almost all the time. But as it grows up, its pattern of sleep changes. It sleeps less and less and stays awake longer, playing or crying or babbling. By adulthood, the pattern is well established; people sleep eight or nine hours a day. Well, not quite that long, for our sleep habits have changed over the last century or so, and we do not get as much sleep as we ought to.

In the eighteenth and nineteenth centuries, people went to bed early, soon after it was dark. They had nothing to do in the evenings, and their sleep habits were fixed by the alternation of day and night, light and darkness. They woke up by daybreak and, thus, they could get nine hours of sleep on an average.

Today, the situation has changed. People, especially in industrialised countries, get less than eight hours of sleep per day; many of them believe that six or six-and-a-half hours of sleep is enough for them. According to biologists and specialists in sleep disorders, a large number of people are not sleeping enough, and this sleep deficit affects their health and their performance.

How did this change in our sleep habits come about? One cause was the introduction of the light bulb. When the electric bulb came into common use, people could work till late in the evening or even till past midnight. As the life of a civilised community became more complex, people began to deprive themselves of sleep in order to squeeze their busy schedule into the late evening hours. Many factories introduced the shift system, by which people work in eight-hour cycles by rotation. A worker who has been working 8.00 a.m. to 4.00 p.m. during one month is asked to work from midnight till 8.00 a.m. during the next month. The human brain cannot adapt easily to such a different sleep time, and as a result, the worker loses his sleep till the new pattern is established.

Millions of people today travel by air across time zones and suffer jet lag in the process. The world has become one big market, and business people have to be constantly travelling; this robs them of their sleep. Even at other times, these men and women have

to stay awake keeping track of market developments in the business capitals of the world, like New York, London and Tokyo. If they fail to monitor the movements of prices in the foreign markets, they will be the losers.

Radio and television must bear their share of responsibility for depriving people of sleep. Even after local TV transmissions have closed by midnight, satellite transmission brings programmes from other transmitting stations across the world throughout the night. Many people get addicted to television and consider themselves compensated for the loss of sleep by being able to watch interesting programmes of entertainment or live telecasts of sports or political events from foreign countries.

Research has shown that the performance of people suffers if they are deprived of sleep. They cannot concentrate, they cannot absorb what they are reading, they cannot make calculations; they make mistakes. Some traffic accidents can be traced to drivers falling asleep while at the wheel. Sleep-deprived people cannot be alert, and this can lead to accidents in factories when such people lose their concentration while monitoring machines.

(contd on p. 85)

* * *

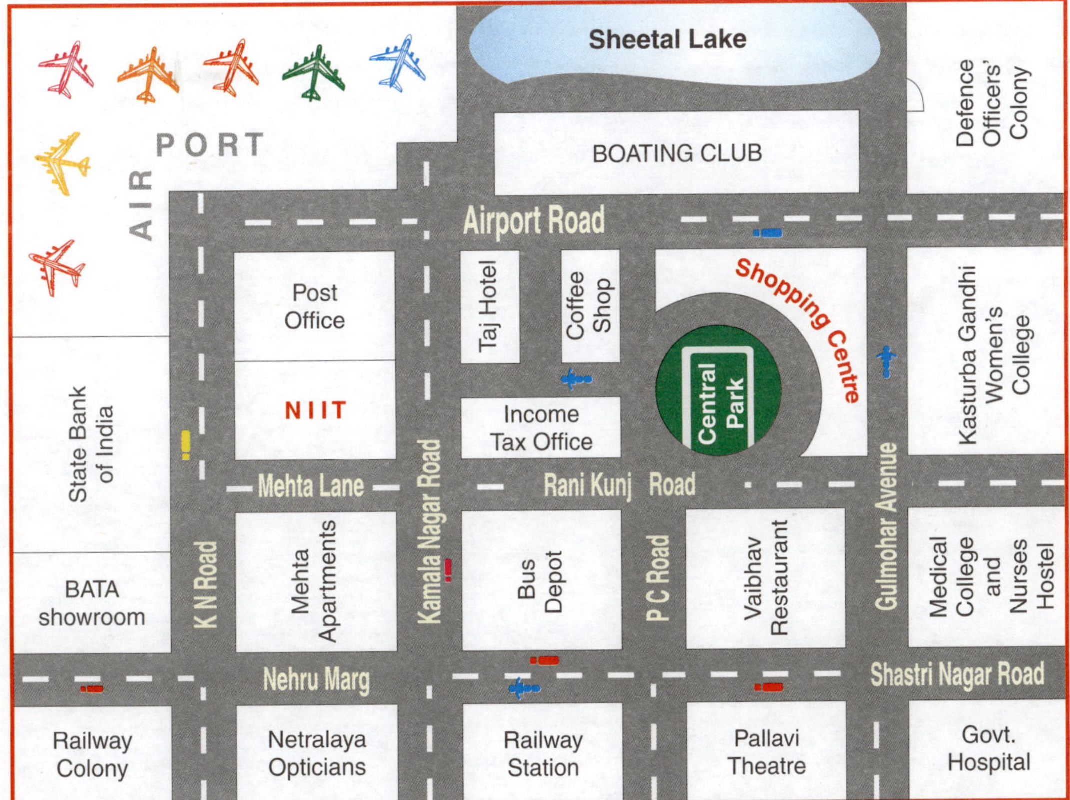

What, then, is to be done to set things right? Obviously, people should learn to sleep more. One way is to take a siesta in the afternoon, as people often do in tropical countries. Extra sleep during weekends can help, but where there has been severe deprivation, it may take a long time to make up for lost sleep. The most sensible thing to do would be to go back to our old-time habits and sleep an hour longer every night. Sleep therapists advise us to take this extra sleep at bedtime in the evening rather than in the morning.

If you find that you are dozing off while doing a routine job or while driving a car, take care; you need to change your sleep habits.

B. *Choose a passage of about 500 words from one of your textbooks and write an abstract of it in about 50 words.*

Environment

WATER: THE ELIXIR OF LIFE

Man has through the ages sought in vain for an imaginary elixir of life, the divine *amrita*, a draught of which was thought to confer immortality. But the true elixir of life lies near our hands. For it is the commonest of all liquids, plain water! I remember one day standing on the line which separates the Libyan Desert from the Valley of the Nile in Egypt. On one side was visible a sea of billowing sand without a speck of green or a single living thing anywhere visible on it. On the other side lay one of the greatest, most fertile and densely populated areas to be found anywhere on the earth, teeming with life and vegetation. What made this wonderful difference? Why, it is the water of the river Nile flowing down to the Mediterranean from its sources a couple of thousands of miles away. Geologists tell us that the entire soil of the Nile valley is the creation of the river itself, brought down as the finest silt in its flood waters, from the highlands of Abyssinia and from remote Central Africa, and laid down through the ages in the trough through which the Nile flows into the sea. Egypt, in fact, was made by its river. Its ancient civilization was created and is sustained by the life-giving waters which come down year after year with unfailing regularity.

I give this example and could give many others to emphasise that this common substance which we take for granted in our everyday life is the most potent and the most wonderful thing on the face of our earth. It has played a role of vast significance in shaping the course of the earth's history and continues to play the leading role in the drama of life on the surface of our planet.

There is nothing which adds so much to the beauty of the countryside as water, be it just a little stream trickling over the rocks or a little pond by the wayside where the cattle quench their thirst of an evening. The rainfed tanks that are so common in South India—alas, often so sadly neglected in their maintenance—are a cheering sight when they are full. They are, of course, shallow, but this is less evident since the water

is silt-laden and throws the light back, and the bottom does not therefore show up. These tanks play a vital role in South Indian agriculture. In Mysore, for example, much of the rice is grown under them. Some of these tanks are surprisingly large and it is a beautiful sight to see the sun rise or set over one of them. Water in a landscape may be compared to the eyes in a human face. It reflects the mood of the hour, being bright and gay when the sun shines, turning to dark and gloomy when the sky is overcast.

One of the most remarkable facts about water is its power to carry silt or finely divided soil in suspension. This is the origin of the characteristic colour of the water in rainfed tanks. This colour varies with the nature of the earth in the catchment area and is most vivid immediately after a fresh inflow following rain. Swiftly flowing water can carry fairly large and heavy particles. The finest particles, however, remain floating within the liquid in spite of their greater density and are carried to great distances. Such particles are, of course, extremely small, but their number is also great and incredibly large amounts of solid matter can be transported in this way. When silt-laden water mixes with the salt water of the sea, there is a rapid precipitation of the suspended matter. This can be readily seen when one travels by steamer down a great river to the deep sea. The colour of the water changes successively from the muddy red or brown of silt through varying shades of yellow and green finally to the blue of the deep sea. That great tracts of land have been formed by silt thus deposited is evident on an examination of the soil in alluvial areas. Such land, consisting as it does of finely divided matter, is usually very fertile.

The flow of water has undoubtedly played a great part and a beneficent one in the geological processes by which the soil on the earth's surface has been formed from the rocks of its crust. The same agency, however, under appropriate conditions, can also play a destructive part and wash away the soil which is the foundation of all agriculture, and if allowed to proceed unchecked can have the most disastrous effects on the life of the country. The problem of soil erosion is one of serious import in various countries and especially in many parts of India. The conditions under which it occurs and the measures by which it can be checked are deserving of the closest study. Soil erosion occurs in successive steps, the earliest of which may easily pass unnoticed. In the later stages, the cutting up and washing away of the earth is only too painfully apparent in the formation of deep gullies and ravines which make all agriculture impossible. Sudden bursts of excessively heavy rain resulting in a large run of surplus water are the principal factors in causing soil erosion. Contributory causes are the slope of the land, removal of the natural protective coat of vegetation, the existence of ruts along which the water can flow with rapidly gathering momentum, and the absence of any checks of such flow. Incredibly large quantities of precious soil can be washed away if such conditions exist, as is unhappily too often the case.

The menace which soil erosion presents to the continuance of successful agriculture is an alarming one in many parts of India, calling urgently for attention and preventive action. The terracing of the land, construction of bunds to check the flow of water, the practice of contour cultivation and the planting of appropriate types of vegetation are amongst the measures that have been suggested. It is obvious that the aim should be to check the flow of water at the earliest possible stage before it has acquired any appreciable momentum and correspondingly large destructive power.

Water is the basis of all life. Every animal and every plant contains a substantial proportion of free or combined water in its body, and no kind of physiological activity is possible in which the fluid does not play an essential part. Water is, of course, necessary for animal life, while moisture in the soil is equally imperative for the life and growth of plants and trees though the quantity necessary varies enormously with the species. The conservation and utilisation of water is thus fundamental for human welfare. Apart from artesian water the ultimate source in all cases is rain or snowfall. Much of Indian agriculture depends on seasonal rainfall and is therefore very sensitive to any failure or irregularity of the same. The problems of soil erosion and of inadequate or irregular rainfall are closely connected with each other. It is clear that the adoption of techniques preventing soil erosion would also help to conserve and keep the water where it is wanted, in other words, on and in the soil and such techniques therefore serve a double purpose.

It is evident however that in a country having only a seasonal rainfall an immense quantity of rain water must necessarily run off the ground. The collection and utilization of this water is, therefore, of vital importance. Much of it flows down into the streams and rivers and ultimately finds its way to the sea. Incredibly large quantities of the precious fluid are thus lost to the country. The harnessing of our rivers, the waters of which now mostly run to waste, is a great national problem which must be considered and dealt with on national lines. Vast areas of land which at present are mere scrub jungle could be turned into fertile and prosperous country by courageous and well-planned action.

Closely connected with the conservation of water supplies is the problem of afforestation. The systematic planting of suitable trees in every possible or even in impossible areas, and the development of what one can call civilized forests, as distinguished from wild and untamed jungle, is one of the most urgent needs of India. Such plantation would directly and indirectly prove a source of untold wealth to the country. They would check soil erosion and conserve the rainfall of the country from flowing away to waste, and would provide the necessary supplies of cheap fuel, and thus render unnecessary the wasteful conversion of farmyard manure into a form of fuel.

The measures necessary to control the movement of water and conserve the supplies of it can also serve subsidiary purposes of value to the life of the countryside. By far the cheapest form of internal transport in a country is by boats and barges through canals and rivers. We hear much about programmes of rails and road construction, but far too little about the development of internal waterways in India. Then, again, the harnessing of water supplies usually also makes possible the development of hydroelectric power. The availability of electric power would make a tremendous difference to the life of the countryside and enable rural economy to be improved in various directions. In particular it would enable underground water to be tapped to a greater extent than at present, and thus help to overcome the difficulties arising from irregularity or inadequacy of other sources of supply.

In one sense, water is the commonest of liquids. In another sense, it is the most uncommon of liquids with amazing properties which are responsible for its unique power of maintaining animal and plant life. The investigation of the nature and properties of water is therefore, of the highest scientific interest and is far from an exhausted field of research.

C.V. Raman

Comprehension

A. *Read the given text carefully and answer the following questions briefly.*

1. Why is water considered the true elixir of life?
2. C. V. Raman says that water in a landscape may be compared to the eyes in a human face. Why?
3. How does soil erosion occur and what are the chief factors that cause it?
4. What are the usual measures used to check soil erosion?
5. What is the measure suggested by C.V. Raman to control the movement of water in order to harness it for useful purposes?
6. Why is the study of the nature and properties of water of the highest scientific interest?

B. *Choose from a, b and c, the correct endings to the following sentences.*

1. The common substance which we call water
   a. is the most potent and most wonderful thing on the face of the earth.
   b. is something that does not contribute to any function on earth.
   c. has very minimal uses and can easily be replaced.
2. When silt-laden water mixes with the salt water of the sea
   a. the salt water pushes the silt away into the sea and the silt becomes useless.
   b. there is no fruitful outcome of this phenomenon and there are no distinct advantages.
   c. there is a rapid precipitation of the suspended matter leading to fertile soil in such areas.
3. India, being a country which has only seasonal rainfall,
   a. has no problem as far as conservation and distribution of water is concerned.

b. has the problem of an immense quantity of water evaporating from the surface of the ground.

c. has the problem of an immense quantity of rain water running off the ground.

4. The most advantageous result of having availability of electric power is that
   a. it allows villages and small towns to be lighted up.
   b. it helps the small farmer to increase his production.
   c. it helps underground water to be tapped to a greater extent than at present.

Vocabulary

A. *Mark the right meanings or synonyms of the words in the sets given below.*

1. stagnate
   a. intimate   b. stimulate   c. vegetate
2. vacillation
   a. indecisiveness   b. oscillation   c. dissimulation
3. enervation
   a. negation   b. exhaustion   c. synergism
4. negate
   a. recapitulate   b. castigate   c. deny
5. abnegate
   a. sacrifice   b. hoard   c. reduce
6. easily tricked
   a. incredulous   b. ingenious   c. gullible
7. inexperienced
   a. credulous   b. naïve   c. credible
8. noble
   a. pusillanimous   b. morally good   c. unanimous
9. frank
   a. ingenious   b. ingenuous   c. intrepid
10. ennui
   a. illness   b. boredom   c. lifelessness

B. *Look up the following words in a dictionary. Find out how each word is pronounced, which syllable of the word is stressed, the part of speech it belongs to (noun, verb, pronoun, etc.), and in case the word has more than one core meaning, identify the sense in which the word is used in the text that you have just read.*

1. draught	2. potent
3. apparent	4. import
5. appreciable	6. harnessing

Grammar

When the verb in the main clause is in the past tense, the verb in the subordinate clause also is usually in the past tense.

I told him that he should be back home.
He said he would be back home after three months.

But this is not applicable always. For example, in:

Copernicus proved that the earth moves round the sun.

what Copernicus said in the past holds good for all time and therefore though 'proved' is in the simple past tense, 'moves' is in the habitual present as it refers to a general truth for all time.
If the verb in the main clause is in the present or future tense, the verb in the subordinate clause may be in the past tense or present tense according to the context.

I think Ravi has written the essay.
I think Ravi wrote the essay.
I shall prove that Ravi wrote the essay.

A. Fill in the blanks with the correct tense form of the verb or the auxiliary in brackets.

1. He gave me as much advice as I ....(need)
2. Whenever I .... there, I remember my mother. (go)
3. Though he came last of all, he .... the first to go. (be)
4. Keep these papers in your cupboard so that they .... be safe. (may/might)
5. He has not come, just as I........... (think)
6. He .... write only if he has a pen. (can/ could)
7. His writings were much better than I ....(expect)
8. There are more books here than I .... (imagine)
9. He talks as if he .... just returned from abroad. (has/ had)
10. We took some food with us so that we did not .... on our way. (starve)

B. The following passage has not been edited. There is one error in each line. Underline each error and write the correction in the space provided. The first correction has been done as an example.

A shoemaker named Simon, who had neither house or land	nor
of his own, lived with his wife and children in the peasant's hut	(1) ______
and earned his living by the work. Work was cheap but	(2) ______
bread was dear, and which he earned he spent for food.	(3) ______
The man and the wife had but one sheepskin coat	(4) ______
among them for winter wear, and even that was worn to	(5) ______
tatters, and this was the second year he had been wanted to	(6) ______
buy sheepskin for the new coat. Before winter Simon saved up	(7) ______
few money: a three-rouble note lay hidden in his wife's box.	(8) ______

Listening

You will now listen to Einstein's lecture, either read aloud to you by your teacher or played on tape. (If necessary, you can ask your teacher either to read the lecture again or play the tape a second time.) As you listen, write either TRUE or FALSE next to each of the statements given below.

1. Einstein praises the progress made by science.
2. Einstein claims that applied science has liberated man from physically exhausting labour.
3. Applied science has many harmful implications during wars.
4. According to Einstein, technical progress is of value only if it helps to solve problems of the organisation of labour and the distribution of goods.
5. Applied science, according to Einstein, has not brought happiness to mankind in the final analysis.

Speaking

Listen to the dialogues that your teacher will play for you on tape and also read their transcripts in your book. Pay attention to the italicised expressions in the transcripts. The dialogues present situations, social and business, where a complaint is being made.

Dialogue 1 (formal)

(Mrs Nair goes to her neighbour, Shamim, to make a complaint.)

Mrs Nair: Good evening, Mr Shamim. *I'm sorry to trouble you, but there's a small problem that I want to speak to you about.*

Shamim: What is it, Mrs Nair?

Mrs Nair: *There seems to be a leak in your bathroom pipe and the water seeps through the roof of our flat downstairs. Could you have the pipe repaired, please.*

Shamim: Oh, I'm terribly sorry. I knew the pipe had a leak somewhere, but I didn't realise that it was causing damage to your flat. Please forgive me. I'll have the pipe repaired immediately.

Mrs Nair: *That's very kind of you, Mr Shamim. I hope you didn't mind my bringing up this matter.*

Shamim: *Oh no, Mrs Nair. I'm glad you brought the problem to my notice. I wouldn't have known about it otherwise.*

Dialogue 2 (formal)

(The new washing machine that Shashi Bajaj bought stops working after being used for just two days. In spite of the calls she makes, the dealer does not send a service engineer to take a look at it. Shashi goes to the company's office to make a complaint to the manager in charge of the customer service division.)

Shashi Bajaj: Good morning, Mr Dutta. *I have a complaint to make.*

Dutta: Good morning, ma'am. Could you tell me what the problem is, please.

Shashi: I bought a Fine Wash fully automatic washing machine from Mayuri, your dealer at Prabhat Nagar, on the 12th of this month. The machine was installed on the 13th. *It ran well for two days but on the third day, it simply stopped working. Mayuri has not responded to any of my calls. I'd like you to help me in getting the piece replaced.*

Dutta: This is most unfortunate, ma'am. I'll speak to the dealer at once. Please don't worry. I assure you that the defective machine will be replaced by a fresh piece before evening. Please accept my apologies.

Shashi: *Thank you, Mr Dutta, for being so understanding and helpful. I'm sorry for having bothered you.*

Dialogue 3 (informal)

(Anil and Afifa are close friends. Anil gets selected to the IPS but forgets to tell Afifa about it. Afifa is hurt and complains to Anil about his behaviour.)

Afifa: Anil, *I'm very upset with you.*

Anil: Why, Afifa, what have I done?

Afifa: *I hear that you have been selected to the Indian Police Service. I'm surprised that you didn't think of telling me about it.*

Anil: Oh Afifa, I'm so very sorry! I don't know why I thought that you were with all our other friends when I broke the news. Do forgive me if you can.

Afifa: *That's all right. These things happen sometimes. I knew you wouldn't deliberately do a thing like that.*

Exercise A

You will now hear on tape some expressions used in both formal and informal situations to make complaints. Listen to each item and repeat it, using the right intonation.

- I'm sorry to trouble you, but there's a problem I'd like to speak to you about.
- It would help if you could have the leaking pipe repaired.
- That's very kind of you.
- I hope you didn't mind.
- I have a complaint to make.
- My new washing machine is not working.
- Your dealer has not responded to my calls.
- I'd like to have the piece replaced.
- I insist on having the piece replaced.
- Thank you for being so understanding and helpful.
- I'm sorry to have bothered you.
- I'm very upset with you.
- I'm very annoyed with you.
- I'm surprised you didn't think of giving me the good news.
- That's all right.
- I guess these things happen.
- Let's just forget it, shall we?

Exercise B

Working in pairs, write and enact the following situations in the form of brief dialogues choosing appropriate expressions from those given above.

1. Mr Nigam has by mistake been sent a huge bill by the telephone department for calls made on another number. He goes to meet the official in charge of billing at the Bharat Sanchar Nigam office in his area and make a formal complaint.
2. Maria finds that her sister has forgotten to feed the parrot that she left in her care while out of station. She calls her on the telephone and complains.

Writing

Writing technical reports

Some useful points to remember

- Technical reports are written on receiving instructions from a person in authority.
- They are investigative in nature for they are written after studying or surveying a subject area, a situation, the working of an industry, etc.
- Technical reports are most often used in making decisions.

- The first step in writing a technical report involves the collection of data through investigations, inquiry, meetings, surveys, etc.
- The second step is to arrange the information in a format used for the purpose.
- The style and tone used in such reports is usually formal.

Look at the format used to write technical reports and note how it is divided into sections.

1. To appear on the front cover
   - **To:** name of the person to whom the report is being sent
   - **From:** name of the person writing the report
   - **Topic or title:** a brief statement of the subject of the survey
   - **Date:** when the report is being submitted
2. Introduction
   - **Terms of reference:** answers the questions 'Who instructed the writer to prepare the report?', 'What was he or she asked to investigate?' and 'When was the report to be submitted?'
   - **Abstract:** a summary often given with long reports so that busy officials get their essential substance through a quick reading
   - **Procedures followed:** how the writer of the report collected the necessary information
3. Findings
   - a concise description of the situation in a simple, direct style
   - problems/strengths/weaknesses
   - conclusions
4. Recommendations
   - solutions
   - advantages of suggested solutions
   - cost implications, requirements, etc.

A technical report must be accompanied by a formal covering letter thanking the person, persons or the organisation concerned for assigning to you the task of making the report and stating your availability for further discussions and clarifications.

Exercises

A. *You are the designs engineer in a bicycle manufacturing company. The general manager has received a new design and a prototype bicycle from a small engineering firm. He has asked you to test the new bicycle thoroughly and send him a report. Write the report in the form of a letter, following the model given in the discussion. Plan your letter carefully. Mention the tests you have carried out and the results. The notes below list some of the features of the new bicycle.*

cheaper – designed to carry more than one person – size reduced to make it lighter and stronger – medium-sized wheels, to gain safety and stability and to reduce cost – hub brakes instead of rim brakes – lamp and bell permanently fixed on the bicycle – low crossbar – adjustable seat height

B. *Look at the following terms of reference forming part of a report.*

To investigate and evaluate the office procedure currently followed in the customer care cell of the Delhi office and recommend ways of streamlining the procedure to make it quicker and more customer-friendly. A committee, consisting of the managers of the Chennai, Delhi and Mumbai offices, was set up to conduct the investigation and submit a report with its recommendations on or before 1 October 2005.

C. *Write similar terms of reference for any one of the following reports.*

1. The management of a newspaper wants to start a weekly magazine and has nominated a committee to make a study of magazine readership in the state.
2. A committee consisting of professors and Education Department officials has been formed to recommend reforms in the examination system.
3. A committee of teachers and students is to study the functioning of the college library.

Inspiration

REACHING FOR THE STARS

Kalpana Chawla, India's first woman astronaut to go into space, was born in 1961 in Karnal to Banarasi Lal Chawla and Sanjyoti. Youngest in a family of four children, Kalpana had two sisters and a brother. Her father's people had come to India from Pakistan during the riots following Partition carrying nothing more valuable with them than their innate optimism and resourcefulness. Although the family was economically comfortable by the time Montu—as Kalpana was fondly called at home—was born, she as well as her brothers and sisters grew up on accounts of the remarkable hard work and perseverance that had got the family where it was. Speaking to *India Today* before the launch of the Columbia in 2003, Kalpana said about her early years as a member of the Chawla family, 'You couldn't lose by working hard, and everyone seemed to follow the rule. It helped instil the notion that no matter what the circumstances, you can indeed follow your dreams.' It is thus easy to understand how the grit and determination so characteristic of the family elders left a deep and lasting impression on young Kalpana.

Growing up as a girl child in Karnal was full of social barriers and restrictions. For one, there was in the place very low value attached to education for girls. Fortunately, conservative as they were, Banarasi Lal Chawla's family gave great importance to academic excellence among all its children—both boys and girls. Kalpana also found immense strength and unfailing support in her mother who believed that one should always do what one loves best. It was Sanjyoti who taught her youngest child to never give up on anything she believed in. Kalpana went to a school that was close to her home, the Tagore Bal Niketan. Though it was not large or among the 'best' in town, the school had a special advantage in that it was headed by a principal who loved children and it had teachers who were caring and deeply committed to their profession. As it turned out to be, her school and teachers went a long way in the shaping of Kalpana, a fact that she remembered with gratitude all her life.

In many ways, Kalpana's years at school were quite similar to those of hundreds of other children growing up in a provincial town in India. On piecing together reminiscences and anecdotes related by friends, teachers and acquaintances, the picture that emerges is that of a shy but cheerful girl with boundless energy and a strong inclination for adventure. Even at a very young age, the small-built girl with dark eyes and a bright smile impressed people around her with her remarkable determination as well as her strong sense of commitment to work and people. Kalpana never topped her class, but her sharp mind and diligence always kept her among the first five. Though she was not really gregarious or an extrovert, her fun-loving, energetic nature made her enjoy organising picnics and outings with her classmates. It was also characteristic of Kalpana to respond with enthusiasm to any challenge or adventure as she did when she learnt to drive a car when barely fourteen years old.

It is clear that Kalpana was always fascinated by aircraft. One of the teachers in her school, Ms Daljeet Madan, recalls how the girl loved making pictures and models of airplanes in her art and craft classes. On her way back from school, Kalpana would often rest against her parked bicycle and watch trainer aircraft land and take off with an expression of joy and wonder on her face. In fact, seeing her passion for flying, her father managed to arrange for his daughter a few joyrides aboard trainer aircraft at the local flying club.

We see another small sign of the direction her dreams would take in Kalpana's memory of what used to be a favourite pastime. On hot summer nights, when the family would sleep in the open on coir cots, Kalpana would lose herself in the endless dark sky scattered with twinkling stars. The sight of the Milky Way and an occasional shooting star would fill the young girl's mind with awe and bring a rush of several basic questions to her curious mind. Many years later, Kalpana remarked that those nights under the star-strewn skies marked the beginning of the deep sense of fascination that she was to always feel for the blue yonder.

By the time Kalpana Chawla left school with an impressive academic record to her credit, she knew with amazing certainty for one so young that she wanted to be an aerospace engineer. Kalpana completed her pre-degree from Dayal Singh College in Karnal and immediately afterwards was selected for admission to Punjab Engineering College (PEC) in Chandigarh. The event caused a furore in the conservative Chawla household that was clearly uncomfortable at the thought of sending Montu outside their town. However, with the calm manner and quiet resolve so typical of Kalpana, she succeeded in convincing her family that her chosen path was one she just had to tread upon.

At the PEC, Kalpana—who had by then decided that she wanted to be a flight engineer and design aircraft—opted to study aeronautical engineering. Again, the principal and teachers at the college tried to persuade Kalpana to change her choice to the streams of civil, electrical or mechanical engineering, which they believed held far better career opportunities for a student as bright as she was. Kalpana, however, was not to be swayed from her carefully made decision and chose to become a part of the small class of eight as its only girl student. Looking back at her years

at the PEC, it appears that it was while she was there that Kalpana had begun to, quietly but surely, chart the course of her destiny. It was indeed remarkable that at each point in her life when she had to make a choice, Kalpana would turn without hesitation or fear towards the more difficult and challenging option. With her indomitable attitude and persistence, she began to get noticed by her teachers and classmates, and soon rose to the top of the class. Her interest and enthusiasm in her subjects of study were unflagging, and it was clear that Kalpana was thoroughly enjoying every moment of the undergraduate course in engineering. This is easy to believe in view of her conviction that it is not only the final destination that is important but also, in equal measure, the journey there. It also agrees with her unchanging opinion over the years that one should enjoy whatever one does in life—a maxim she held close to her heart.

Friends in college remember Kalpana Chawla as being a very pleasant and unassuming person who could talk to everybody on whatever their interests happened to be. She spent most of her time in the classroom, the library or laboratory, but this did not stop her from participating in the annual sports day and other college functions, or in the activities of its Aero and Astro Society. At the PEC, Kalpana learnt about aircraft materials, propulsion and theoretical aerodynamics, which gave her a strong foundation for her future years of study and which also proved to be of great value to her much later when she became an astronaut.

As she neared the end of her undergraduate course, Kalpana Chawla started exploring possibilities for continuing her studies in the United States of America. After considering many places, Kalpana finally decided to attend the University of Texas at Arlington (UTA). She felt that the university had excellent teaching and research opportunities to offer and was both excited and overjoyed when she was admitted to its graduate programme. Once again, her family was unhappy at the thought of sending the young woman outside India, but Kalpana persisted until she convinced them that her decision to continue her studies abroad was indeed the best possible course open to her. Thus in 1982, when she left her small hometown to travel to Texas, Kalpana Chawla took yet another of the seemingly small steps that was to lead her to the grand finale of the dream she had nurtured in her heart for so long a time.

Once in Arlington, Kalpana plunged with amazing ease into the tightly packed routine of the American MS programme, which while being very demanding also offers a high degree of academic freedom.She was soon recognised in the university for her strong ambition and academic credentials. In the words of Don Wilson, her thesis guide at Arlington, 'My first impression was that she was a quiet and shy girl who was intimidated by her surroundings. But she adapted very well and came across as a very high-spirited individual with a burning desire to succeed.' Most of Kalpana's time on campus was spent in classrooms and the library. She would also spend long hours in the laboratory, sometimes working late into the night, long after everyone else had left.

In December 1983, Kalpana married French-American Jean-Pierre Harrison who was among the first friends she had made on her arrival in the United States. Her conservative family was understandably upset about the marriage, but as on other occasions in her life when she took decisions on her own, Kalpana won their approval and blessings with her firm faith in what she believed was best for her. It was simply wonderful how, as she moved on in life, Kalpana always managed to take her family along without allowing the smallest rift or the slightest trace of rancour to mar her relations with them.

After completing her master's programme, Kalpana moved with her husband to Colorado, set in the breathtaking Rocky Mountains. At first, she enrolled for a Ph.D in mechanical engineering but shortly afterwards decided to shift to aerospace engineering that had always been her passion. The fact that Kalpana made a request for a change in discipline knowing only too well the risks involved in doing so is a clear mark of her inner strength and clarity of purpose. Miriam, a dear friend at Colorado, speaks of how the shy girl would amaze everybody by defending her stand on academic topics or explaining her point of view to her teachers and senior research scholars in the department with courage and self-confidence.

Shortly after completing her Ph.D in 1988, Kalpana Chawla joined the NASA Ames Research Center in California. Her work involved the simulation of complex airflows around aircraft such as the Harrier in 'ground effect'. While at the research centre, she also applied to the NASA Space Centre to become an astronaut, thus giving expression to her ultimate dream. Meanwhile another exciting opportunity came to her in 1993 when she was given a job as vice president and research scientist with Overset Methods, Inc, in the Silicon Valley.
The position was a challenge and also a recognition of her competence, for Kalpana was put in charge of developing and implementing techniques for aerodynamic optimisation.
Her other major area of work was related to the reproduction of the effect of the loss of gravity on body parts. The research was done in the hope that its findings would help reduce the problems that astronauts commonly face in space because of not being able to coordinate their physical movements.

During the time between 1992 and 1994, Kalpana became a student of the Abhinaya Dance Academy in San Jose where she learnt Bharatanatyam. She had always been passionate about dancing and so when she found a way of realising her dream, the truly multi-faceted woman did not allow her busy schedule or commitments at work to deny her the rare chance to do so.

People who knew Kalpana at the dance school remember her as being quiet about her achievements and as being always ready to listen to what others had to say about their lives.

Finally, after what would have seemed an eternity to the incredibly single-minded woman, Kalpana was informed by NASA that she was to appear for an interview and medical evaluation that could lead her to the job of an astronaut. It was the finest of achievements in itself because she was among the 122 aspiring astronauts chosen from a total of 2962 applications. Kalpana, never one to rest on her laurels or take success for granted, worked hard to prepare herself for the interview. In doing this, she paid special attention to improving her public speaking skills, an area where she thought that she may be found wanting. Eventually Kalpana Chawla became one of the nineteen candidates selected to be members of NASA's fifteenth batch of astronauts. It was an honour that would have been beyond the wildest dreams of a person coming from a small town in distant India. However, for Kalpana the selection was not a chance happening but a logical culmination to years of taking tiny, measured steps—and focusing intently on just one at a time—in a steep climb that took her to the very summit of her long-time goal. The young woman was the pride of her family and nation for Kalpana had indeed travelled a great distance, both literally and figuratively, and she took the glory with astounding calm and humility.

In March 1995, Kalpana moved to Houston with Jean-Pierre, who had proved to be a supportive co-voyager in the course of her difficult journey, to begin her tough training programme at the NASA Center. The training comprised an introduction to all NASA centres, instruction in land and sea survival as well as in operating aircraft. Further, there were months spent in high-fidelity simulators and under zero-gravity conditions. At the end of a year, Kalpana was selected as a crew representative in the NASA Astronaut Office Extra-vehicular Activity and Computer Branches where her work included testing space shuttle control software.

In November 1997, Kalpana was given the chance she had dreamed about and lived for all her life. She was to go into space as one of the six crew members on board the Columbia shuttle's STS-87 mission. As mission specialist, Kalpana represented the diverse scientific disciplines of physics, chemistry, astrophysics, aerospace engineering, geology, space sciences and computer science. Kalpana was also assigned the job of the prime robotic arm operator, which required her to operate the manipulator arm for launching and retrieving satellites. Being a mission specialist further meant that she had to monitor experiments conducted on board and perform Extra-Vehicular Activities. All this was in addition to assisting the commander and pilot and keeping a check on the shuttle systems for any problems that could arise.

Kalpana was never to forget her first sight of the earth from the shuttle thousands of miles in space. Apart from the sheer wonder of the experience, the astronaut was deeply impressed by the philosophical import of the realisation that our planet is really only a very small part of the vast universe. She was also struck by the thought of how vulnerable it is to complete destruction unless the people living on earth make a serious effort to save its environment and natural resources. The feeling remained with her and Kalpana, who had always been a nature enthusiast, never missed a chance in all the rest of her life to speak about the urgent need to take care of our habitat.

It is indeed a mark of Kalpana's fineness as a person that in spite of her hectic schedule at NASA and the pressures of her life there, she never forgot her friends or the institutions that she had been associated with. She always kept in touch and took them along in her path of glory. Thus, Kalpana took care to present autographed mementos that she had carried with her on her first space flight to all her friends as well as to her school, pre-degree and engineering colleges and to the universities that she had attended in the United States. Kalpana was a loyal friend who believed in lasting relationships and she steadfastly stood by people she had been close to at different times in her life. Together with this, there was in the young woman an intense yearning to give back a part of what she had gained to society and to all those who had inspired her. It was possibly this desire that got her involved with a programme allowing two students from her school, the Tagore Bal Niketan, to visit the NASA facilities every year. In fact, before making what was to be her final trip, Kalpana had made careful plans to sponsor a young student to a university in South Africa.

Other honours came to Kalpana in the years following her first voyage aboard the Columbia shuttle. She was first appointed crew representative for shuttle and station staff crew equipment and later chosen to head the Astronaut Office's Crew Systems and Habitability section. Kalpana could have at this point in her life chosen the relatively easy path of being ground crew, just as some two years ago she could have opted to stay on in Silicon Valley and earn an impressive salary without having to risk her life and safety. The fact that at each of the two junctures in her life when she could have very well opted for a softer alternative, Kalpana willingly chose the more difficult and challenging path speaks volumes for Kalpana's essential calibre and sincerity. Thus, she was selected as a crew member for the STS-107 launch, again aboard the Columbia space shuttle. The purpose of the 16-day mission was mainly to conduct research on micro-gravity. The experiments were to provide a better understanding of the physical processes at work on the earth and they were a part of a collaborative effort made with scientists based in different countries of the world.

Soon after what was described as a perfect launch, the members of the crew began the work that had been assigned to them. Kalpana conducted experiments on earth sciences, life sciences and physical sciences. As flight engineer she also kept a close and careful watch over the shuttle's systems. Kalpana was carrying some mementos that she wanted to take back to family and friends at the end of the flight and also a collection of CDs containing some of her favourite music. A few of the pieces were used by the NASA Space Center in Houston as wake-up music. In her communication to the space centre on the day Ravi Shankar's *Prabhati* was played, Kalpana said, 'Good morning, Linda, and thank you very much. That's a favourite piece of music of mine and I think it is titled *East Meets West*. And it fits this setting too as we are going around the earth all day long. And seeing it all really makes you feel it is one and the same.'

On 1 February 2003, the Columbia was ready to re-enter the earth's atmosphere. Kalpana's family and friends were waiting at Cape Canaveral, where the shuttle was to land, and at her Houston home. Suddenly and without warning, all communication with the Columbia snapped when it was at a height of 207,135 feet in the sky. The white trail of the shuttle streaking into the earth's atmosphere, which had been visible on television screens and to people in some areas, broke up into a series of white spots, and this was followed by a loud boom. A tragedy beyond words had occurred. The Columbia carrying seven crew members on board had disintegrated while making its re-entry into the earth's atmosphere. There were no survivors.

Kalpana Chawla was a truly remarkable woman who presented a rare combination of a brilliant mind and an intensely humane spirit. Her courage to dream about what would have seemed unattainable to most as well as her determination and relentless perseverance in striving to achieve her goal were qualities that led her to an incredibly accomplished and meaningful life. The astronaut has left behind for her family, her nation and the world an invaluable legacy of faith in the ability of human beings to surmount all odds and find success in following a trail of continued seeking and adventure. Aeronautical engineer, research scientist, space traveller—Kalpana Chawla will indeed be remembered as all these but, even more significantly, she will remain a part of the world's heritage for the extraordinary will power and daring that she showed in her attempt to reach for the stars.

Comprehension

A. *Read the given text carefully and answer the following questions briefly.*

1. How did Kalpana Chawla's family background contribute to the shaping of her personality?
2. What was the first barrier that Kalpana as a child came up against?
3. Write a brief note on early indications in Kalpana's life of the future that awaited her.
4. What lasting effect did the view of the earth from space have on Kalpana?
5. According to those who knew her, when faced with options, Kalpana always chose the more difficult and challenging one. Give two instances from her life to substantiate this opinion.
6. Kalpana Chawla was 'a rare combination of a brilliant mind and an intensely humane spirit'. Discuss.

B. *Choose from a, b, c, d and e the correct endings to the following sentences.*

1. Kalpana Chawla was fascinated and awed even when she was very young by
   a. sleeping in the open.
   b. things far away.
   c. the colour blue.
   d. the thought of going to engineering college.
   e. the stars in the night sky.
2. Though as a child Kalpana was hardworking and determined, she was always
   a. rather weak in her studies.
   b. at the top of her class.
   c. friendly and talkative.
   d. unfriendly and unhelpful.
   e. keen on helping her family economically.
3. When Kalpana was selected to Punjab Engineering College, her parents
   a. were angry.
   b. stopped her from joining the collage.
   c. were afraid that she might become an astronaut.
   d. were reluctant to send her away from Karnal.
   e. were delighted that their daughter had been selected.
4. Kalpana's firm belief that it is not the final destination that is important but the journey there
   a. made her overconfident.
   b. made her believe in destiny.
   c. made her work with enthusiasm and interest.
   d. shows that she was very intelligent and capable.
   e. brought her honour and fame.

Vocabulary

A. *Match the words, taken from the above text, in Column A with the meanings in Column B.*

A	B
1. convince (verb)	a. to break up into very small pieces
2. pastime (noun)	b. courage and determination
3. furore (noun)	c. to make someone believe something
4. resolve (noun)	d. something you do to pass your time in a pleasant way
5. disintegrate (verb)	e. decision
6. grit (noun)	f. a sudden burst of anger or excitement among many people

B. *The abstract noun 'clarity' corresponds to the verb 'clarify'. Give abstract nouns corresponding to the following verbs.*

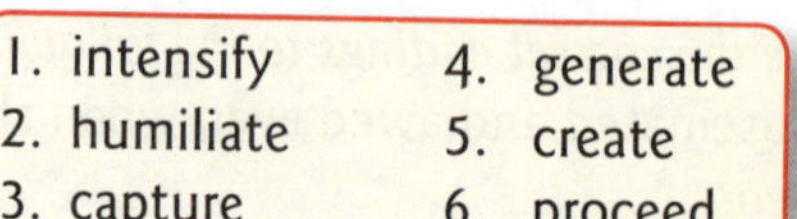

1. intensify
2. humiliate
3. capture
4. generate
5. create
6. proceed

C. *Find words in the above text that are antonyms of the following words.*

1. pessimism	2. short-lived	3. introvert
4. mental	5. common	6. bondage

Grammar

A. *Read the passage below and answer the questions that follow according to the instructions given after each.*

She was worried about her son. The boy had been sleeping badly of late. His nights were troubled with fearful dreams. He had felt a shadow follow him constantly. At first he had tried not to pay it any attention. But one day he had heard its name mentioned and the name was Death. The boy had told her all this one day. She had been scared, but had tried to brush aside his fears, which were also her fears. 'Why should you be afraid?' she had asked him: 'You are young, strong, healthy. There's nothing wrong with you.'

But the boy had shaken his head and she had seen the terror in his eyes.

1. Why was the mother worried?
   (Answer in the simple past tense)
2. What troubled the boy?
   (Answer in the simple past tense)
3. What had he felt following him constantly?
   (Answer in past perfect tense)
4. What had he tried doing at first?
   (Answer in past perfect tense)
5. What was it that he had heard one day?
   (Answer in past perfect tense)

Conditional clauses contain conditions which are not fulfilled. For example, look at these sentences.

If he had listened carefully, he would not have lost his way.

If you had come earlier, you would have seen the documentary film.

If you exercise regularly, you will keep fit.

You will not be given a second chance if you make a mistake.

If I pass my examination I shall give you a treat.

B. Here are some broken sentences. Column A has the first part of the sentence and column B has the second part. Join the parts together and write out each sentence correctly.

A	B
1. If I have time	a. you will play a good game.
2. If you eat all those sweets	b. it will be cooler.
3. If you practise regularly	c. I will practise my music.
4. If it rains	d. I will come.
5. If you send me a message	e. you will surely be ill.
6. If the fire engine had not come	f. you would have got all the news.
7. If you had received my letter	g. I will let you go out, not otherwise.
8. If the fever comes down	h. the building would have been completely burnt to the ground.

It is usual among users of English to add what are called *question tags* in conversation. One makes a statement and immediately asks the listener if the statement is correct. An interesting point about question tags is that when the statement is in the affirmative, the tag is in the negative and vice versa.

You are a dancer, aren't you?

You aren't a dancer, are you?

They enjoyed your music, didn't they?

They didn't enjoy the music, did they?

C. Add question tags like the above to the statements below.

1. You are writing the examination.
2. You have been working hard.
3. Anuradha has been doing yoga for years.
4. He is wasting paper.
5. Naina was hoping all would be well.
6. The players were winning.
7. Engineering is popular among students.
8. Medicine comes next.

Listening

You will now listen to a farmer's success story. After you have listened to the tape for the first time, read the following statements about the farmer on the tape and choose the correct responses to each of them. (You can put a √ mark against each correct choice.)

1. The underlying theme of the success story that you just heard is to
   - encourage farmers to do both crop raising and dairy farming.
   - narrate the difficulties of Narain Singh in selling the milk.

- discourage farmers from raising crops.
- to show that agriculture and animal sciences are inter-related.

2. In your opinion, the interviewer is a(n)
   - sales representative of milk products.
   - agricultural extension worker.
   - educated farmer.
   - a student of agriculture and animal sciences.
3. Narain Singh had
   - fifteen buffaloes.
   - eight buffaloes.
   - three buffaloes.
   - fifty buffaloes.
4. Narain Singh used his farm lands to raise
   - cereals and fodder.
   - cereals only.
   - fodder.
   - cereals and wheat.
5. The milk collection centre in his village gave relief to Narain Singh because
   - it gave him tremendous profit.
   - it saved him the trouble of walking long distances to sell milk.
   - it enabled him to obtain information on milk and dairy products in his own village.
   - it helped him to collect the dues that the milk agency owed him every month.

Speaking

Listen to the dialogues that your teacher will play for you on tape and also read their transcripts in your book. Pay attention to the italicised expressions in the transcripts. The dialogues present situations that call for congratulating, expressing sympathy and offering condolences.

Dialogue I

(Satish's essay on conservation of natural resources wins the first prize in an international competition organised by the UNESCO. His thesis supervisor, Dr Neeru Das, congratulates Satish on his achievement.)

Dr Neeru Das: Satish, I just heard the wonderful news. *Congratulations on your remarkable achievement.*

Satish: Thank you very much, Dr Das. It is all because of the encouragement and help that I have always got from you.

Dr Neeru Das: Not entirely. *It's a result of your own hard work and perseverance. Satish, you really deserve this honour. Everyone in the department is really proud of you. I'm sure you will keep up the good work.*

Satish: Thank you, ma'am. It's very kind of you.

Dialogue 2

(Sudha does not make it to the university basketball team in spite of the months of hard work she has put in. Her coach, Abraham, expresses his sympathy and consoles Sudha.)

Abraham: Sudha, *I'm sorry about your not getting selected for the university basketball team. I can understand just how you feel after all the hard work you put in.*

Sudha: Sir, this is really terribly disappointing! I don't know where I went wrong.

Abraham: Look Sudha, *you mustn't let yourself be disheartened by this small setback. I just know how good you are. If it will make you feel better, the selectors had a very difficult time in coming to a final decision on the team. You must realise that these things are all a part of the game and accept what has happened with true sportsmanship.*

Dialogue 3

(Tanya has lost her grandfather. Her friend, Meher, comes to offer his condolences.)

Meher: Tanya, *I'm truly sorry about your grandfather. I understand how shattered you feel at the moment.*

Tanya: I can't believe he is gone forever. I'll always miss him so badly.

Meher: Yes, Tanya, *your grandfather was indeed a special person. Nobody who met him could fail to adore him. It is a great loss, but we must be grateful for the fact that he went peacefully in his sleep without the least suffering.*

Tanya: Thank you, Meher. I don't know how I could have coped without all of you.

Exercise A

You will now hear on tape some expressions used in both formal and informal situations to congratulate somebody on an achievement, to express sympathy and to offer condolences. Listen to each item and repeat it, using the right intonation. Remember that these are situations that call for sincerity and genuine feeling and in the absence of these, the words become mere clichés.

- Congratulations!
- We are proud of you.
- You really deserve this honour.
- Very well done! Keep it up!
- I'm sure this won't happen again.
- I've no doubt that you'll do much better next time.
- I just got the sad news. This must be a terrible blow to all of you.
- It is a great loss indeed.
- You must be brave.
- Remember that we are all with you.
- I'm sorry about what happened.
- You mustn't let this depress you.

Exercise B

Working in pairs, write and enact the following situations in the form of brief dialogues choosing appropriate expressions from those given above.

1. Prabha is in bed with jaundice. She will not be able to take the final examinations in two subjects. Her aunt visits her to express sympathy and comfort her.
2. Professor Prasad has won ICAR's Scientist of the Year Award. His colleague Dr Susie Sapra congratulates him.
3. On hearing about the death of Steve's mother, Rajesh visits his colleague to offer his condolences.

Writing

Preparing a résumé

Some useful points to remember

- The résumé (pronounced *re-zyu-may*), as the curriculum vitae (CV) is called in American English, is another term for a biodata and it is sent with a short letter of application for a job or for admission to a course of study.
- It is a brief account of your personal details, your education and the work experience that you have had.
- Your résumé must be neatly printed or typed and appealing to the eye.
- Under the heading 'academic qualifications', you can include school, college and university attended, years and degrees earned, class or grade point average obtained and details of participation in co- and extra-curricular activities.
- Under 'Work experience' you can give details of organisations where you worked earlier, dates and responsibilities.
- If necessary, you can list any other skills that you may have and that you consider relevant to the job. For example, you may want to mention that you helped develop software for hostel fee accounting.
- Use action verbs rather than nouns to describe your experience and skills. For example, instead of saying that you have some experience as a 'counsellor' with high school students, you could say that besides teaching your subject, you also 'counsel' your high school class regularly.
- Avoid giving information that is not relevant to the application.
- Personal information such as marital status, family and hobbies need not be included in a résumé unless asked for.

Here is a specimen résumé.

Résumé

Name:	**Vandana Verma**
Address:	80/A Creek Lane Kolkata 700 050
Telephone:	2829037
Nationality:	Indian
Date of birth:	7 June 1970
Academic qualifications:	
• 1990–1993	Diploma in Mechanical Engineering with 58% marks
• 1990	Passed the Higher Secondary examination from South Point School with 60% marks
• 1988	Passed the Secondary School examination from Kendriya Vidyalaya, Bagdogra Cantt with 72% marks
Other qualifications:	Diploma in computer applications
Work experience:	**June 1997–February 1998:** Working as technician in G. S. Industries, Mumbai **Job profile:** Communicating technical information from engineers to workers: guiding workers working on difficult technical projects **February 1995–May 1997:** Worked as an apprentice at Technical Solutions, Kolkata **Job profile:** Practical exposure to machine work, performing routine technical work relating theory to practice

Exercise

A. *Using the above résumé as a model, prepare one for an older relative or friend who is employed.*

Writing a statement of purpose

Some useful points to remember

- A statement of purpose is a type of essay that you have to write when you apply for admission to a foreign university.
- The statement of purpose gives you an opportunity to show how you are unique and also how you can add value to your class.
- Avoid abstract statements and high-sounding clichés such as 'I want to improve the condition of people around me.' Instead, you can give an example of something you have done, even on a small scale.
- If the college does not specify the length of the essay, keep your essay to one or two pages, with single spacing.

- The opening lines of the essay must catch the attention of the reader, without appearing to be trivial. In the opening paragraph itself you can say how your background prepared you for the field of study you hope to enter.
- Then you can refer to your education and write about any experiences that you feel are relevant to the course of your choice. You could mention, for example, that you worked in a social or voluntary organisation where you got interested in the subject.
- Your previous academic performance, especially that in the last examination taken, is important. Therefore, in case it is not good, try to give a credible reason for your inadequate grades.
- Doing some research on the institution will help you make specific statements about how the programmes there could help you achieve your academic goals.
- You must also be able to show clearly the relevance of the programme to your future plans.
- After you write your statement of purpose, revise it and write again till you get an impressive, compact essay.
- Follow the principles of composition and also pay attention to your language. Avoid slang and abbreviations. Do not use language that sounds artificial or pseudo-literary.
- Edit and proofread your essay several times. No errors of grammar or punctuation should be left uncorrected.
- Do not submit an essay from the Internet as your own.

Exercises

A. *Write an application essay in answer to the question 'What will your contribution be to student life in St John's College?'*

B. *James Joyce said, 'Mistakes are the portals of discovery.' Describe an event that you view as a failure or a mistake on your part. What did you learn from the experience?*

Language games

To make your English class fun, here is a bag of assorted language games.

A. *The encircled word(s) in the following sentences have a request each. Help them if you can.*

1. 

Mani, the shepherd boy, took good care of the sheep that his grandfather had left with him at the farm.

2. The baby was sleeping in the cradle.

3. A warm reception was given to the visiting dignitaries.

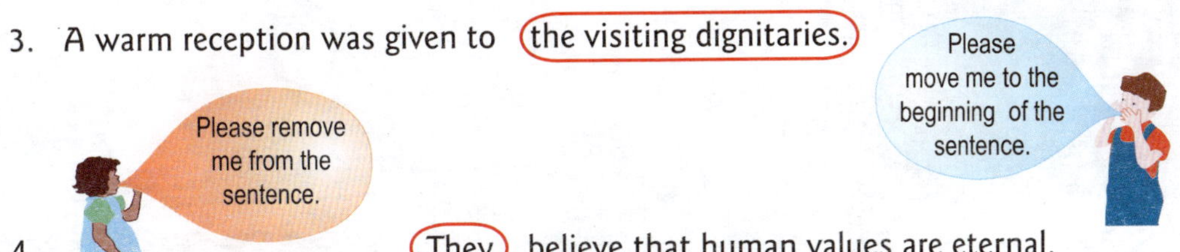

4. They believe that human values are eternal.

B. *There are two bridges leading from one part of a road to the other. Tick the one you will choose to travel by in 1–3 below.*

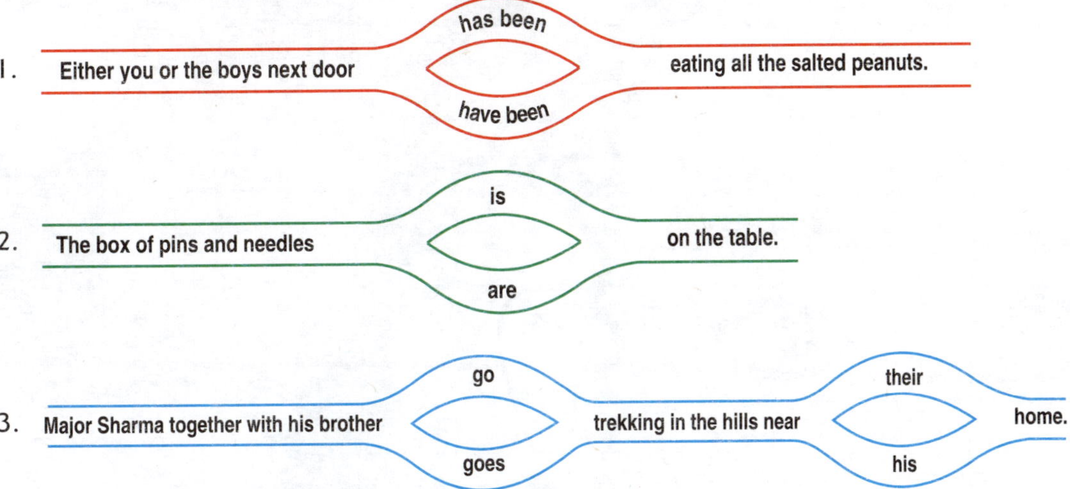

C. *Can you describe each of the words in pink circles by arranging the words in blue circles around it in the right order?*

1.

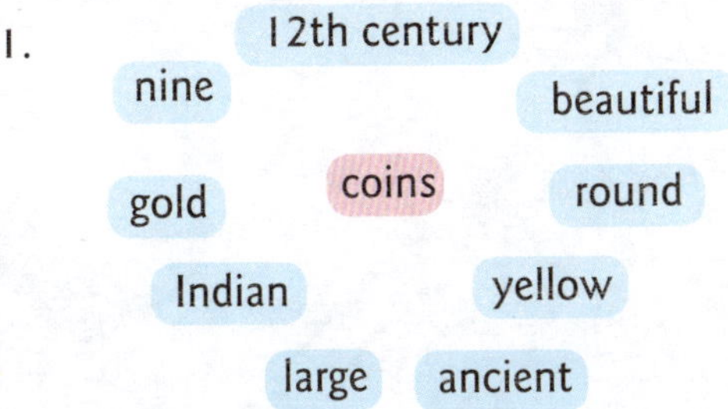

2.

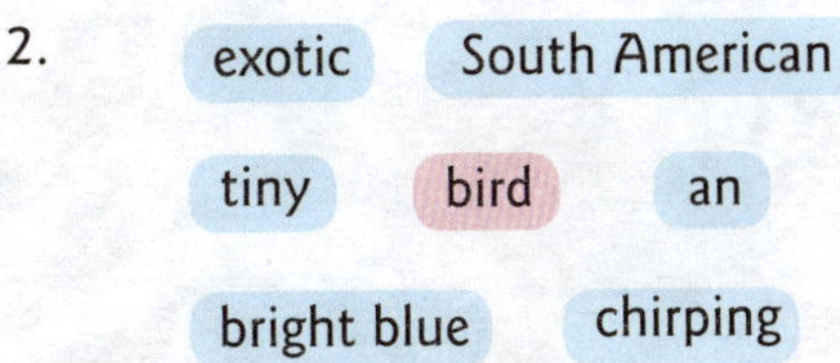

Human Interest

A SERVICE OF LOVE

When one loves one's Art no service seems too hard.

Joe Larrabee came from the Middle West with a genius for painting. As a child of six, he drew a picture of the town pump with an important citizen passing it in a hurry. This effort was framed and hung in the drugstore window. At twenty he left for New York with a flowing necktie and a small capital.

Delia Caruthers came from the South. She was so promising a singer that her relatives collected a small amount for her to go to New York and learn music.

Joe and Delia met in a studio where a number of art and music students had come together to discuss their art. Joe and Delia fell in love and in a short time were married—for, when one loves one's Art no service seems too hard.

Mr and Mrs Larrabee began to live in a flat. It was a lonely place. But they were happy; for they had their Art, and they had each other. And my advice to the rich young man would be: sell all you have, and give it to the poor—for the happiness of living in a flat with your Art and your Delia.

Joe was painting in the class of the great Magister—you know his fame as a painter. His fees are high; his lessons are light. Delia was studying under Rosenstock—you know his fame as a musician.

They were mighty happy as long as their money lasted. Their aims were very clear. Joe would learn very soon to paint pictures that old gentlemen with side-whiskers and thick purses would fight with one another in his studio for buying. Delia was going to master the piano and fill concert halls all over the country with people who would pay twice the usual rates to hear her play.

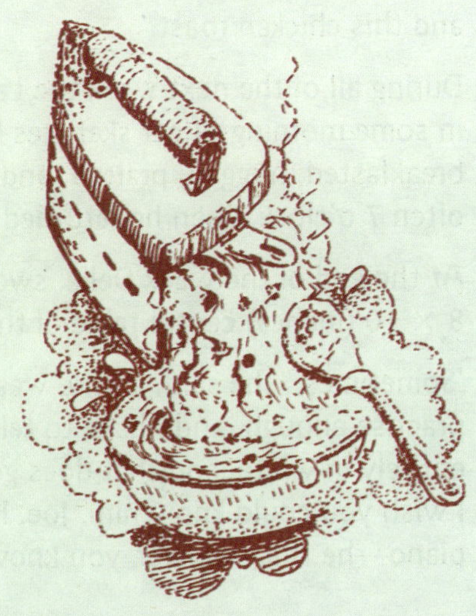

But the best, in my opinion, was the home life in the little flat—the warm chats after the day's study; the pleasant dinners and fresh, light breakfasts; the exchange of hopes; the help and love they gave each other.

But after a while Art became weak. Everything going out and nothing coming in, as some people say. There was no money to pay Mr Magister and Mr Rosenstock their fees.

When one loves one's Art no service seems too hard. So, Delia said she must give music lessons to buy their food.

For two or three days she went out looking for pupils. One evening she came home in high spirits.

'Joe, dear,' she said, happily, 'I have a pupil. And, oh, the loveliest pupil. General—General A.B. Pinkney's daughter—on Seventy-first Street. Such a splendid house, Joe, you should see it. Oh, Joe, I never saw anything like it before.'

'My pupil is his daughter Clementina. I dearly love her already. She's a delicate thing—dresses always in white; and the sweetest, simplest manners! Only eighteen years old. I have to give three lessons a week; and just think Joe, five dollars a lesson! I don't mind it a bit; for when I get two or three more pupils I can continue my lessons with Mr Rosenstock. Now, don't look so unhappy, dear, and let's have a nice supper.'

'That's all right for you, Dele,' said Joe, opening a tin of peas, 'but how about me? Do you think I'm going to let you work for wages while I enjoy myself painting? No. I can sell papers or break stones and bring in a dollar or two.'

Delia came and hung about his neck.

'Joe, dear, you are silly. You must keep on at your studies. I hadn't left my music and gone to work at something else. While I teach I learn. I am always with my music. And we can live as happily as rajahs on fifteen dollars a week. You mustn't think of leaving Mr Magister.'

'All right,' said Joe, reaching for the vegetable dish. 'But I hate your giving lessons. It isn't Art. But you're a dear to do it.'

'When one loves one's Art, no service seems too hard,' said Delia.

'Magister praised the sky in that drawing made in the park,' said Joe. 'And Tinkle gave me permission to hang two of them in his window. I may sell one if the right kind of a rich art-collector sees them.'

'I'm sure you will,' said Delia, sweetly. 'And now let's be thankful for General Pinkney and this chicken roast.'

During all of the next week the Larrabees had an early breakfast. Joe was very much interested in some morning-effect sketches he was doing in the Central Park, and Delia packed him off, breakfasted, hugged, praised, and kissed at 7 o'clock. Art is a charming mistress. It was most often 7 o'clock when he returned in the evening.

At the end of the week Delia, sweetly proud but tired, threw three five-dollar bills on the 8 × 10 (inches) centre table of the 8 × 10 (feet) sitting room.

'Sometimes,' she said, a little wearily, 'Clementina tries my patience. I'm afraid she doesn't practise enough, and I have to tell her the same thing so often. And then she always dresses entirely in white, and that does get boring. But Gen. Pinkney is the dearest old man! I wish you could know him, Joe. He comes in sometimes when I am with Clementina at the piano—he is a widower, you know—and stands there pulling his white beard.

"And how are the lessons getting on?" he always asks.

'I wish you could see the drawing room, Joe, and the rugs! And Clementina has such a funny little cough. I hope she is stronger than she looks. Oh, I really am getting very fond of her, she is so gentle and noble. Gen. Pinkney's brother was once Minister to Bolivia.'

And then Joe, with pride, drew forth a ten, a five, a two and a one—all new dollar notes—and laid them beside Delia's earnings.

'Sold that watercolour of the tower to a man from Peoria,' he announced joyfully.

'Don't joke with me,' said Delia, 'not from Peoria!'

'All the way. I wish you could see him, Dele. Fat man with a woollen muffler and a bald head. He saw the sketch in Tinkle's window and thought it was a windmill at first. He bought it anyhow. He ordered another—an oil sketch of the Lackawanna goods yard to take back with him. Music lessons! Oh, I guess Art is still in it.'

'I'm so glad you've kept on,' said Delia, heartily. 'You're certain to succeed, dear. Thirty-two dollars! We never had so much to spend before. We'll have oysters tonight.'

'And champagne,' said Joe.

On the next Saturday evening Joe reached home first. He spread his eighteen dollars on the dining table and washed what seemed to be a great deal of dark paint from his hands.

Half an hour later, Delia arrived, her right hand tied up in a shapeless bundle of wraps and bandages.

'What happened?' asked Joe after the usual greetings. Delia laughed, but not very joyously.

'Clementina,' she explained, 'said we must have a Welsh rabbit after her lesson. She is such a strange girl. Welsh rabbits at five in the afternoon! The General was there. You should have seen him run for the dishes Joe, as if there wasn't a servant in the house. I know Clementina isn't in good health; she is so nervous. In serving the rabbit she spilled a great lot of it, boiling hot, over my hand and wrist. It hurt awfully, Joe. And the dear girl was so sorry! But Gen. Pinkney!—Joe, that old man nearly went mad. He rushed downstairs and sent somebody out to a drugstore for some oil and things to bind it up with. It doesn't hurt so much now.'

'What's this?' asked Joe, taking the hand tenderly and pulling at some white threads beneath the bandages.

'It's something soft,' said Delia, 'that had oil on it. Oh, Joe, did you sell another sketch?' She had seen the money on the table.

'Did I?' said Joe, 'just ask the man from Peoria. He got his goods yard today, and he isn't sure but he thinks he wants another view of the park and a view on the Hudson river. What time this afternoon did you burn your hand, Dele?

'Five o'clock, I think,' said Delia, sadly. 'The iron—I mean the rabbit came off the fire about that time. You ought to have seen Gen. Pinkney, Joe, when . . .'

'Sit down here a moment, Dele,' said Joe. He drew her to the sofa, sat beside her and put his arm across her shoulders.

'What have you been doing for the last two weeks, Dele?' he asked.

She looked at his face for a moment or two with an eye full of love, and murmured a word or two about Gen. Pinkney; but at length down went her head and out came the truth and tears.

'I couldn't get any pupils,' she confessed. 'And I couldn't think of your giving up your lessons; so I got a place ironing shirts in that big Twenty-fourth Street laundry. And I think I did very well to invent both General Pinkney and Clementina, don't you, Joe? And when a girl in the laundry set down a hot iron on my hand this afternoon I was inventing that story about the Welsh rabbit all the way home. You're not angry, are you, Joe? And if I hadn't got the work you mightn't have sold your paintings to that man from Peoria.'

'He wasn't from Peoria,' said Joe, slowly.

'Well, it doesn't matter where he was from. How clever you are, Joe—and—kiss me, Joe—and what made you ever suspect that I wasn't giving music lessons to Clementina?'

'I didn't,' said Joe, 'until tonight. I sent up this cotton waste and oil from the engine-room this afternoon for a girl upstairs who had her hand burned with an iron. I've been working the engine in that laundry for the last two weeks.'

'And then you didn't' ...

'My buyer from Peoria,' said Joe, 'and Gen. Pinkney are both creations of the same art—but you wouldn't call it either painting or music.'

And then they both laughed, and Joe began:

'When one loves one's Art no service seems—'

But Delia stopped him with her hand on his lips. 'No,' she said, 'just "When one loves." '

O. Henry

Comprehension

A. *Read the given text carefully and answer the following questions briefly.*

1. How did Delia earn the fifteen dollars that she threw on the table at the end of the week?
2. How did Joe earn his eighteen dollars?
3. Why did Joe need to wash his hands so hard before Delia returned?

4. At what point in the story did Delia and Joe guess the truth about the other?
5. Why was Delia's laughter not very joyous when she tried to explain the fact that her hand was in a bandage?
6. Is this a story about great art or great love?

B. *Choose from a, b, c, d, e the correct endings to the sentences.*

1. Joe and Delia hoped to earn enough to live on comfortably
   a. but learnt that this is possible only with hard work.
   b. but also needed to love each other deeply.
   c. were very foolish in their judgments.
   d. and gave music lessons to well-to-do students.
   e. but learnt that this is not at all easy to do.
2. Clementina and her father General Pinkney
   a. were very fond of music.
   b. played the piano regularly.
   c. were creations of Joe's imagination.
   d. were imaginary characters invented by Delia.
   e. paid Delia handsomely.
3. Joe was not able to
   a. work efficiently.
   b. sell his paintings.
   c. paint well because he had not studied art.
   d. play the piano at all.
   e. buy good food like oysters and champagne on his earnings.

Vocabulary

See how some phrasal verbs are used.

To give: You know that *to give* someone something means to hand over something to someone or to provide someone with something you own or have. But the phrasal verb *to give up* means to admit that you are defeated or that you cannot do something you hoped you would do.

When you *give away* a secret or an advantage you reveal a secret or information that you should keep to yourself.

To *give off* or *give out* (a smell or a gas or heat) means that it produces it (a smell or a gas or heat) and sends it out into the air.

To keep: You *keep* something safely *in* your cupboard. But to *keep on* doing something means to continue to do something repeatedly.

When you *keep to* a rule or a plan or a path or road you do what you must do and not move away from it.

You *keep up* with someone moving with you when you are moving at the same speed as him (or her or them).

To come: You say *'come on'* to someone to encourage them so that they continue to do well. When you *come across* someone or something you meet him (or her or them or it) by chance. When you *come through* a difficult situation you have survived it and recovered from it.

A. *Fill in the blanks below with the correct phrasal verbs given above and rewrite the sentences.*

1. Aman ran so fast that Venkat could not .... with him.
2. The Chawlas went through hard times when they migrated to India but they .... their difficulties and are now happy and well settled.
3. .... John. You've got to win! You're almost there!
4. I'm wearing a wig to hide my baldness. Don't .... my secret and embarrass me, please.
5. I haven't met Anu for a long time. If you .... her please give her my good wishes.

B. *Joe had a genius for painting and wanted to be an artist. Delia could sing very well and wanted to be a musician. Match the phrases in column A with their one-word substitutes in column B. Also use a dictionary to find out the meaning of the extra word in column B.*

A	B
1. one who takes up the study of humankind	a. chiropodist
2. one who compiles a dictionary	b. connoisseur
3. one who treats ailments of the feet	c. clincher
4. one who knows several languages	d. anthropologist
5. one who is an expert in matters of taste	e. lexicographer
	f. polyglot

Grammar

'I'm so glad you've kept on,' said Delia heartily. 'You're certain to succeed, dear ...'

In the above sentence, the narrator of the story has used direct speech, that is, speech directly from the speaker. (Note the inverted commas or quotation marks, sometimes called speech marks.)

The same speech could be reported indirectly, as if the message is reported to one by a third person.

Delia said that she was glad he had kept on and added that she was certain he would succeed.

Note that in the second case where the writer uses indirect or reported speech, no speech marks (inverted commas/quotation marks) are used. They are not necessary. So conversation can be reported directly or indirectly when a writer writes a story.

A. *Change the following to direct speech.*

She told Joe that sometimes Clementina tried her patience. She said that she was afraid she didn't practise enough and that she has to tell her the same thing often. She also complained that Clementina always dressed entirely in white and that this did get boring.

B. *Change the following to indirect speech.*

'I have a problem,' said the student to the teacher, 'in not being able to take any lecture notes from you. At junior college we were given definite outlines to follow and study for examinations.' Her instructor seemed amused. 'Why do you think you learn only from lecture notes?' he asked.

C. *Read the passage below. A word has been omitted in each line. Mark the omissions with a ʟ and write the omitted word in the space provided. The first omitted word has been inserted as an example.*

Peter Mark Roget, ʟ biography still appears in the front of the Thesaurus, whose
was born in London in 1779. He moved his family to Edinburgh (1) ______
at fourteen and entered university there, where he studied medicine. (2) ______
He graduated the medical school at nineteen and began to publish (3) ______
significant research papers tuberculosis of the lungs. In 1805, he (4) ______
took a position as a physician at the Public Infirmary at Manchester. (5) ______
That when he began compiling lists of words to help him achieve (6) ______
precision his presentations. From 1808 to 1840 he concentrated on (7) ______
medicine and, in the of a successful medical career, he discovered (8) ______
the optical illusion known as persistence of vision.

Listening

Work in pairs and follow the steps mentioned below.

- You will hear a lecture on mutation. As you listen to it for the first time, determine the purpose of the lecture.
- Try and listen to the tape without asking for it to be stopped, the first time. This will help you to understand the general purpose of the lecture (the gist).
- After you understand the gist of the lecture, make sure that you understand the details of the lecture. To help you do this you can ask for the tape to be played two or three more times.
- As you listen, make sure that you make notes of the different types of mutation that are referred to in the lecture.

A. *Choose the correct answer. The lecture that you are listening to is about*

1. the harmful effects of mutation.
2. the different types of mutagens in nature.
3. the structure of the nucleotide.
4. the different types of mutation.

B. *Determine the technical term given to the agent that causes mutations. Choose the correct answer from the following options.*

1. purine
2. mutagen
3. pyrimidine
4. DNA sequence

Write your answer here: ....

C. *As you listen to the lecture for the second time, listen to the definition of mutation. Now complete the following sentence which defines mutation.*

Mutation is any change brought about in the base .... of the

....

D. *Work in pairs. Listen to the lecture a third time. The boxes below are already labelled. They are the two different types of mutation: spontaneous and induced mutation. As you listen to the lecture a second or third time, write the essential characteristics of both spontaneous as well as induced mutation, in the table below.*

Spontaneous mutation	Induced mutation
1. _______________	2. _______________
_______________	_______________
_______________	_______________
_______________	_______________

(Keywords: exposure/natural/artificial/mutagens)

E. *Continue to work in pairs. Here is a list of items. As you listen to the lecture again, mark and circle the items which are physical mutagens.*

1. mustard gas	7. x-rays
2. nitrous acid	8. colchicine
3. temperature	9. gamma rays
4. formaldehyde	10. alpha rays
5. beta rays	11. UV rays
6. infra-red rays	

Speaking

Listen to the dialogues that your teacher will play for you on tape and also read their transcripts in your book. Pay attention to the italicised expressions in the transcripts. The dialogues present situations that call for making a suggestion, offering advice and persuading.

Dialogue 1

(Kamala drops in at the local youth club to watch a group of young people rehearse for a play they plan to put up shortly.)

Kamala: That was very entertaining. I enjoyed every minute of the play.

Maya: Thank you, Kamala, for sitting through our rehearsal.

Nasir: Any suggestions, Kamala? We have been at this for so long and have stopped seeing things clearly.

Kamala: *Well, first I suggest that you could think of another title for the play. I don't think the present title is either interesting or suitable.*

Maya: That's a good suggestion. What's your second suggestion, Kamala?

Kamala: *In my opinion, Maya, the character of the old woman whom you play could appear at the end of the play* to say why she behaved as she did. *Do you think it will be possible?*

Nasir: Why not? We'll try that one out. Anything else, Kamala?

Kamala: No, that's all. I really feel you have a wonderful play there.

Maya: Thanks a lot, Kamala! You have been of great help.

Dialogue 2

(Mrs Leela Pai finds her neighbour Ms Preet Hemchandani anxious about her father's illness.)

Mrs Pai: Hello, Preet! Why do you look so anxious?

Preet: Hello, Mrs Pai. Do come in. I'm very worried about father's fever. It just doesn't seem to be coming down. The doctor is not available on Sundays. I don't know what to do.

Mrs Pai: Look Preet, *let me offer you some advice. There is no need to worry yourself sick.* Your father is on antibiotics, and the infection will come under control in a day or two. Meanwhile, *you could try applying a cold compress on his forehead. You must remove that thick blanket and cover him with a light cotton sheet instead. Also, remember that it is important for him to have as much fluids as you can possibly get inside him. However, don't give him anything too cold.*
Sit by his side for at least a few minutes whenever you can and, please, do appear cheerful. Don't you worry, Preet. Mr Hemchandani is going to be his old self in another three or four days. As for now, please don't hesitate to call me if you feel you need my help.

Dialogue 3

(Mallika is going to move to a suburb, away from the noise and pollution of the city where she has lived for many years. She tries to persuade her friend, Farida, to do so too.)

Mallika: *Farida,* did I tell you that I am moving soon to Green Park colony, which is about 20 km from the city?

Farida: Oh! That's so far!

Mallika: You are mistaken, Farida. It's not really as far as you think it is. In fact, *why don't you consider moving there yourself?*

Farida: Well, I really don't think I would like the idea of staying so far from the city.

Mallika: Look, Farida, *could I persuade you to go along with me and see the place for yourself?* It's just a fifteen-minute drive from here. The road to the place is wide and open, with hardly any traffic. There are shops, schools, a bank, a post office and two nursing homes around the colony. Besides the greenery is amazing! *I'm sure you'll decide to move there as soon as you set eyes on the place. Why don't you have a look at the colony?*

Farida: All right, Mallika, I'll go with you today. You really know the art of persuading people, don't you?

Exercise A

You will now hear on tape some expressions used in both formal and informal situations to offer suggestions, to advise or to persuade. Listen to each item and repeat it, using the right intonation.

- I suggest you repeat these expressions twice each.
- I think you should repeat these expressions as often as you can.
- Let's repeat these expressions for practice.
- Why don't we repeat these expressions a few more times?
- I really advise you to repeat these expressions several times.
- You should repeat these expressions in order to perfect them.
- They ought to repeat these expressions if they wish to speak fluently.
- Why don't you try repeating these expressions?
- Do try repeating these expressions.
- Could I persuade you to repeat these expressions as many times as possible?

Exercise B

Working in pairs, write and enact the following situations in the form of brief dialogues choosing appropriate expressions from those given above.

1. Madhuri finds her brother, Manu slipping in his studies. She advises him on how he could pull himself up again.
2. Bhatia gives suggestions to his junior colleagues on how to promote a new brand of health drink.
3. Manohar persuades his friends to visit an exhibition of Indian art.

Writing

Memorandums

Some useful points to remember

- The memorandum, or memo, is an important and much-used form of business communication.
- They are used to announce changes, ask for information and respond to requests.
- They differ from business letters in some important ways.
- Memos are most often used within an office or a business house.
- The salutation and the complimentary close are omitted.
- They have a format that is different from that of letters.
- The body of the message is written in a clear, direct style.
- Routine memos are very short and to the point.
- Longer memos can be divided into paragraphs, with headings if necessary.
- A memo should contain only the necessary information and there should be no repetition.
- Confidential or sensitive information is not communicated in memos.
- A conclusion can be used to suggest further action or to recommend some step.
- If there are attachments sent with the message, these should be mentioned at the bottom of the memo.

The format of a memo consisting of a heading and a message is given below.

(Heading)
Date:
From:
To:
Subject:

(Message)

Look at the different parts of the specimen memo.

MEMORANDUM

Date: 2 October 2005

From: Dean of Student Affairs

To: Mr P. K. Roy, Principal

Subject: Students' Union Elections

The schedule for holding the Students' Union elections was discussed at the meeting of the faculty yesterday. The schedule is listed below.

Task	Date
Filing of nominations	10–15 October 2005
Last date for withdrawal of nominations	20 October 2005
Scrutiny of nominations	25 October 2005
Voting	30 October 2005
Announcement of results	2 November 2005

30 October 2005 will be a holiday for the college.

Exercises

A. *The items in the following memo are in jumbled order. Arrange them in the correct order and label their parts as in the above format.*

1. Service books should be completed well before the date of retirement.
2. 9 January 2005
3. Gratuity payment
4. To: The Accounts Officers
5. Staff members should be paid their gratuity on the day of their retirement.
6. From: The General Manager
7. The payment should be made by demand draft, preferably drawn on the bank of the receiver's choice.

B. *As works manager in a factory, write a memo to the supervisor regarding a rescheduling of the night shifts in the factory. Instead of 10 p.m. to 6 a.m., the shift will work from 9 p.m. to 5 a.m. The other shifts too have been rescheduled accordingly.*

C. *You are Safety Officer in Badri Engineering Company Pvt. Ltd. One of the workers in the company fell from a moveable ladder and had to be hospitalised. The fall was caused by his own carelessness—he had used the ladder without placing wooden blocks at its foot. Send a memo to all the supervisors in the company about instructing workers on the following:*

- moveable ladders to be used carefully
- wooden blocks to be used to fix ladders
- workers to make sure legs are fixed before using ladder
- workers to check ladder instructions in the office.

Media
IAF drops relief supplies over Jaffna
THE HINDU
TeX: A free text-processing tool
Business Line
Gold that went through fire
HINDU
ence on TEX software
BusinessWeek
GLOBAL WARMING
French MPs on religious
Hindustan Times
BJP rejects VHP brand of Hindutva
JIM ROGERS
HOT COMMODITIES
HINDU NATIONALISM
&
Future of the Indian Polity
HINDU NAT
The Future of the

FREEDOM OF THE PRESS

AS I write these words, on May 3, World Press Freedom Day, I am reminded that 12 journalists have been killed just this year, according to the Committee to Protect Journalists, a New York-based independent non-profit organisation. All over the world, journalists are jailed, attacked and harassed every day.

Throughout the world, World Press Freedom Day, observed on May 3, serves as an occasion to inform the public of violations of the right to freedom of expression and as a reminder that many journalists brave death or jail to bring people their daily news. Freedom of the press is the mortar that binds together the bricks of freedom - and it is also the open window embedded in those bricks, through which we can all see the world.

The day marks the anniversary of the Declaration of Windhoek, a statement of principles drawn up by African journalists calling for a free, independent and pluralistic media in their continent and throughout the world. The declaration, adopted in 1991 at a seminar organised by the United Nations and UNESCO in Windhoek, Namibia, affirms that a free press is essential to the existence of democracy and a fundamental human goal.

A free press is one of the most essential components of a democratic society. And there is no longer any serious debate about the proposition that democracy is essential for social and economic development.

There can be little argument that information and freedom go together. The information revolution is inconceivable without political democracy, and vice versa. Already, the spread of information has had a direct impact on the degree of accountability and transparency of governments around the world.

There is widespread recognition that restraints on the flow of information directly undermine development. Global interdependence means that those who receive and disseminate information have an edge over those who curtail it. The consequences are apparent in all fields of human endeavour.

The new hallmarks of development are the ability to receive, download and send information through electronic networks, and the capacity to share information, including not only newspapers and journals, but also online web sites – without censorship or restrictions. Thus developing countries need to open up to the outside world, liberalise the mass media, and resist government control and censorship of information.

This year the United Nations is organising two major events that will stress the centrality of press freedom. The World Electronic Media Forum, convening in Geneva from December 9 to 11, will bring together media executives and practitioners from developed and developing countries, as well as policy makers, to discuss the role of the electronic media in the information society.

The forum will contribute to the only global summit this year – the World Summit on the Information Society, which will be held in Geneva from December 10 to 12, 2003, with a second phase in Tunis in 2005. Freedom of the press will be a major focus of this first-ever global summit on the subject of the information society.

The summit's draft Declaration of Principles stresses 'the commitment to democracy and good governance as well as the existence, in accordance with the legal system of each country, of independent, pluralistic and free mass and other communication media'. If the draft is adopted, world leaders will commit themselves to freedom of expression and guarantee the plurality of information.

The information society of the 21st century can thrive only if citizens are provided with full information to allow democratic participation at all levels. The summit will engage the media as indispensable key participants of the information society, and will, we hope stress the role of press freedom as vital to democracy and good governance.

The summit should also help promote the creation of domestic content, in line with the local culture and in the local language. Cultural diversity and pluralism are essential to an inclusive information society. The 'digital divide' is not only a technological one, but also a content divide that penalises developing countries. The two concepts—diversity of content and press freedom—can and need to go together.

New digital technology offers great possibilities for enhancing traditional media and combining them with new media. Moreover, traditional media, and especially radio and television, remain the sole form of access to the information society for much of the world's population, including the very poor and the illiterate.

Perhaps this is the newest challenge for the United Nations – to work to bring access to information, and the empowerment it offers, to all the world's people. Only then will equity and equality be truly brought to the information revolution. Only then will the world's poor and underprivileged have a real way out of the darkness that shrouds their voices, and their hopes.

[Shashi Tharoor, *The Hindu*, 4 May 2003.]

Comprehension

A. *Read the given text carefully and answer the following questions briefly.*

1. What is the significance of the World Press Freedom Day observed on 3rd May?
2. Why was this day chosen as the World Press Freedom Day?
3. How do you think the spread of information has an impact on the degree of accountability and transparency of governments around the world?
4. What are the new areas of development in the dissemination of information?
5. What are the aims and intentions of the World Summit on the Information Society?
6. How does access to information bring about empowerment?

B. *Choose from a, b and c the correct endings to the following sentences.*

1. If there is restraint on the flow of information
   a. there is development in all spheres of life.
   b. freedom and awareness develop.
   c. development is undermined.
2. Full information is required for citizens
   a. in order to provide democratic participation.
   b. in order to provide forums for debate.
   c. in order to compete with other democratic nations.
3. The newest challenge for the United Nations is
   a. to help in the dissemination of information worldwide.
   b. to work to bring access to information worldwide.
   c. to convince governments to spread information.
4. One of the major focuses in the World Summit on the Information Society will be
   a. creation of domestic content in line with local culture.
   b. freedom of the press as vital to democracy and good governance.
   c. democracy and legal systems.

Vocabulary

Tick the only misspelt word in each group.

a. grammer	b. parallel	c. conscience	d. pursuit
a. wierd	b. seize	c. cease	d. achieve
a. pursue	b. pastime	c. exhillarate	d. kidnapped
a. preceed	b. exceed	c. accede	d. proceed
a. accessible	b. permissible	c. irresistable	d. irritable
a. analyse	b. argument	c. assistant	d. comparitive
a. persistent	b. resistent	c. leisure	d. perseverance

Grammar

A. *Rewrite the following complex sentence as a set of simple sentences, each containing only one finite verb.*

> Though it trembled with emotion which he restrained with some effort, Anton found his voice, so that his careful, somewhat pedantic phraseology for which the famous astronomer was noted, did not abandon him.

B. *Here are several simple sentences. Combine them into one complex sentence, without the use of the conjunction 'and'.*

> The postmaster's salary was meagre. He had to cook for himself. He had also to cook for a village girl. She was an orphan. Her name was Ratan. She was about twelve or thirteen. It seemed unlikely that she would get married.

C. *Rewrite the following complex sentence so as to have a set of simple sentences, each comprising one finite verb.*

> The postmaster who was a Kolkata boy was a fish out of water in a village like this, where his office was in a dark thatched hut with a pond next to it which was scummed over with weeds and jungle all around.

D. *Combine the sentences below into one. (Do not use the conjunction 'and'.)*

> A peasant went out. He went out early one morning. He went out to plough. He took with him his breakfast. It was a crust of bread.

Listening

A. *You will now listen to a conversation on shrink-wrapped seeds. As you listen to the conversation on tape, fill in the answers to the following questions.*

1. As you listen to the conversation, first of all decide how many people are talking on the tape.
   How many? ....
2. Also find out the name of the person who is anchoring this presentation on the radio.
   The anchor's name is ....
3. What is the name of the scientist who talks about her invention?
   The name of the scientist is ....
4. Which country is she from?
   The name of the country is ....

B. What are they talking about? Listen to the tape once again and do as directed below.

1. Try and match the meanings given in the second column of the table on the next page with the term, 'shrink-wrapping of seeds' given in the first column.

shrink-wrapping of seeds	a. shrinking seeds and wrapping them with something b. using a polymer that has been shrunk to wrap the seeds in c. using a polymer to wrap the seeds in d. shrinking both the seed and the polymer that the seed is wrapped in e. seeds are wrapped in polymer and then are treated with heat

2. Complete the following statement by choosing one of the options given below the incomplete statement. (Tick the right answer.)

Statement: Seeds are shrink-wrapped in order to help the farmer combat ....

a. fungi and other diseases.
b. the wet and cold soil conditions which are detrimental to the development of the seeds that have been planted.
c. dry and desiccated soil conditions.
d. fungal attacks and other diseases when seeds are planted in cold and wet soil.
e. the dry conditions when seeds are planted in dry soil.

3. How is it that shrink-wrapping does not hinder the growth of the seeds planted into the ground? Choose an appropriate answer from the four statements below.

a. The farmer is supposed to pull out the seeds and manually remove the wrapping.
b. When the earth warms up, the plastic also warms up and water enters it and it falls apart.
c. When the earth warms up, the heat of the earth causes the plastic coating to fall apart.
d. When the earth warms up, the seed starts growing and its bigger size causes the polymer to fall apart.
e. When it rains, the water enters the plastic causing it to fall apart.

Speaking

Listen to the dialogues that your teacher will play for you on tape and also read their transcripts in your book. Pay attention to the italicised expressions in the transcripts. The dialogues present situations that call for polite forms of expressing agreement and disagreement and also for interrupting a speaker to seek some clarification.

Dialogue I

(Anju, Jessie and Siddique are discussing the idea of a cultural show they plan to organise for an orphanage where Anju's mother is a committee member.)

Anju: I'm glad you both agreed to help me organise a cultural show for 'Aashraya'. My mother is very happy at the thought of the children having a wonderful evening.

Jessie: It's a pleasure, Anju. I'm sure we can put together something exciting that will keep the young ones glued to their seats.

Siddique: The next step is to think of what kind of programme we should have. I think we could have a play in Hindi done by a good theatre group.

Anju: Yes, *I quite agree with you*. That would interest the children. Besides, it would be an opportunity to introduce them to the delights of theatre.

Jessie: *I'm sorry, but I'll differ on that.* A long play will make the children restless and even bored.

Siddique: *Perhaps you're right.* Listen, since the show is going to happen a day before Deepavali, how about having a programme of Indian music and dance on a stage lit up with tiny diyas?

Anju: *That sounds lovely, but I'm afraid I can't accept the idea of having diyas burning so close to the two hundred children packed into a tiny auditorium.*

Jessie: *You're right*, Anju, we really can't take any risks. But what would you say to our having tiny electric bulbs and also to our having the programme in the open?

Anju: In that case, *I think Siddique's suggestion is great.*

Dialogue 2

(Professor Bakshi is lecturing on human evolution in his anthropology class. Adela raises her hand to get his attention.)

Dr Bakshi: ....and so we share a common ancestor with gorillas and chimpanzees. We ...

Adela: *Excuse me, sir. I'm sorry to interrupt, but I remember* reading that we are closer in terms of our genetic makeup to chimps than we are to gorillas. Is that true?

Dr Bakshi: Yes, that's absolutely right. We separated from gorillas about ten million years ago and from chimpanzees, our closest relatives, about seven million years ago.

Adela: *I have another doubt, sir.* Is the theory supported by genetic evidence?

Dr Bakshi: A good question! The answer to that is yes. Over 98 per cent of our DNA is the same as that of the chimpanzees and about 97.5 per cent is the same as that of the gorillas.

Adela: *Thank you, sir.*

Exercise A

You will now hear on tape some expressions used in both formal and informal situations to express agreement and disagreement, and to seek clarification on something. Listen to each item and repeat it, using the right intonation.

- I quite agree with you.
- Perhaps you're right.
- I'm afraid, I'll differ with you on that point.
- I'm sorry, but I can't agree with you there.
- I'm afraid, I can't accept the idea.
- You're absolutely right.
- Excuse me. I'm sorry to interrupt, but I have a doubt that I'd like you to clarify.
- Pardon me for interrupting, but is it true that ....?

Exercise B

Working in pairs, write and enact the following situations in the form of brief dialogues choosing appropriate expressions from those given above.

a. Two persons discuss the issue of euthanasia. They agree on some points and disagree on others.

b. Ms Anjali Majumdar is giving a talk on the first topic in your physics textbook. You have a doubt and would like Ms Majumdar to explain a point she has made before she continues her lecture. You ask for clarification politely.

Writing

Information transfer

Some useful points to remember

- Information in verbal form can be made clearer and easier to understand by presenting it in graphic or pictorial form.
- Pictorial representation has many advantages:
  - allows quick and easy viewing of a large amount of data
  - quicker to locate required information in a graphic than in a written text
  - data relating to a long period of time or to a large number of people can be effectively summarised
  - convenient to use in making comparisons involving large amounts of data:
- The different types of graphic representation you could use to supplement your writing are: tables, bar charts, maps, graphs, pie charts, tree diagrams, flow charts and pictograms.
- When you need to use a graphic form of communication, choose a form that will present your data clearly, accurately and in an interesting manner.
- When information is presented graphically, you should be able to interpret or analyse it.
- Transferring information from textual to graphic form and, conversely, from pictorial to verbal form are both important and useful skills.

Exercises

A. *Look at the following pictures showing the production of natural rubber. Below the pictures there are sentences describing the process, step by step. But the steps are arranged in a jumbled order. Rearrange the sentences to match the sequence of the pictures, so that you get a clear description of the process.*

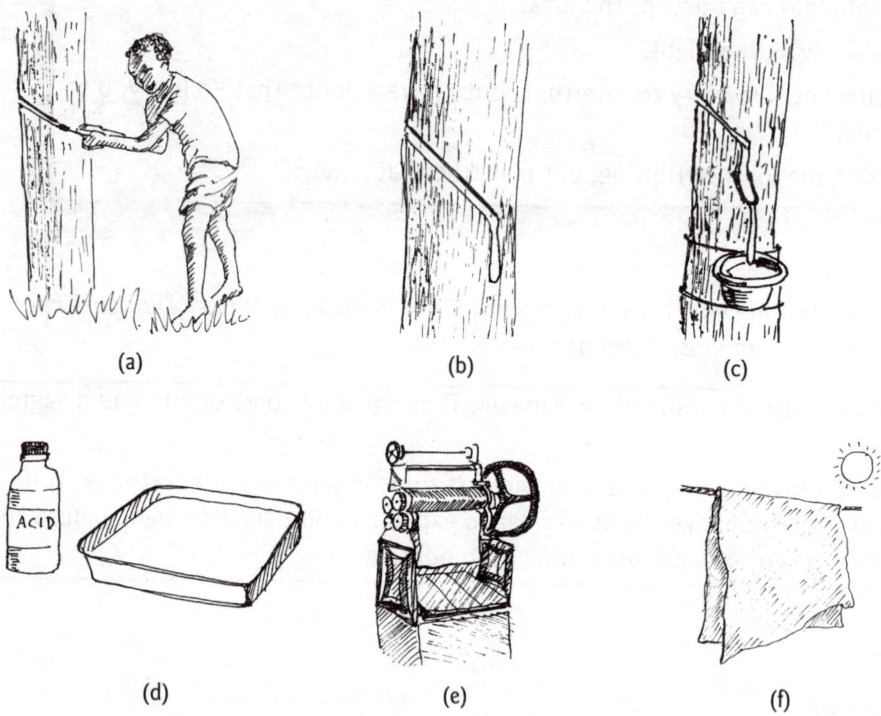

(a) (b) (c)

(d) (e) (f)

1. Latex flows down the groove.
2. Rollers are used to remove moisture and press the latex into sheets.
3. Then it is poured into a basin, and dilute acid is added. By its action, the latex coagulates into a cake-like sheet.
4. After being exposed to smoke in a smoking chamber, the dark-coloured sheets are dried in the sun.
5. A collecting cup is placed below the groove and latex flows into the cup. About three hours later, a tapper collects the latex from each cup and takes it to the processing centre.
6. A tapper cuts a groove on the tree trunk at an angle pointing downwards.

B. *The government of India has announced the introduction of a public distribution system for essential commodities. The system will comprise the following stages. Write a short account of the system with regard to wheat or rice.*

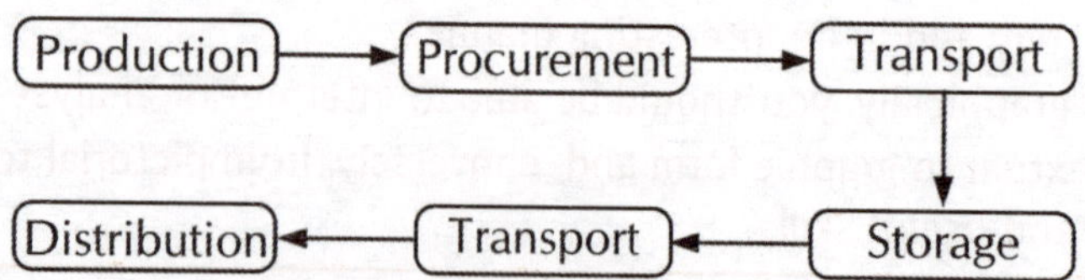

C. *Refer to the notes that you made on fibres in unit 4 ('The Gold Frame') and present the information in a tree diagram.*

D. *Here is a component bar chart that depicts the pass percentage in two degree colleges in the years 2001–2005. Study the bar chart and write a brief note comparing the performance of the two colleges.*

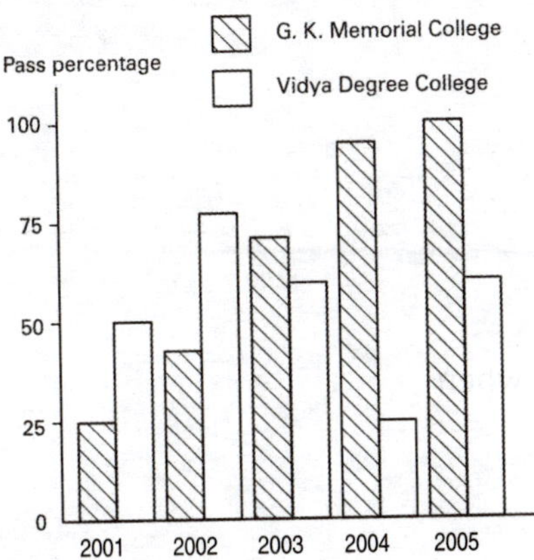

TAPESCRIPTS

Unit 1 Listening A

1. pace; 2. thin; 3. speak; 4. mantle; 5. prism; 6. when

Unit 1 Listening B

1. I am sorry about the pain.
2. Could you thread it for me?
3. The doctor removed a sliver of glass from the wound.
4. How could you miss that tone?
5. I like Pavan's frugal way of living.
6. That's not a very clean sheet.

Unit 2 Listening

A. couch – couch B. assign – assign C. propel – propel D. threw – threw
E. balm – balm F. stale – stale

Unit 3 Listening A

1. 'baggage; 2. de'mand 3. ˌfif'teen 4. pos'sess 5. de'fect
6. 'register 7. ˌunder'stand 8. ˌdisap'point

Unit 3 Listening B

1. 'democrat
   de'mocracy
   ˌdemo'cratic
2. 'demonstrate
   de'monstrative
   ˌdemon'stration
3. 'photograph
   pho'tographer
   ˌphoto'graphic
4. bac'teria
   bacˌteri'ology
   bacˌterio'logical

Unit 4 Listening

1. Ravi has been given a 'permit to import steel.

2. I hope you will not ob'ject to the noise.
3. They decided to sur'vey the situation.
4. The camel took the man across the 'desert.
5. Let's pre'sent this painting to Sheila.
6. It was a 'perfect evening.

Unit 5 Listening A

Mr Gujral: Hello, Seema. It's nice to have you back. How did the holiday go?

Seema: Hello! It was wonderful. Kanya Kumari is lovely in December.

Mr Gujral: What was the weather like?

Seema: Well, it wasn't hot and it didn't rain either except for two days when . . .

Mr Gujral: That must have kept you in the hotel. What a pity!

Seema: Oh, it was nothing more than light showers. Ma and I visited an old palace that has been renovated by the Archaeological Survey of India. We also spent time in a local art museum.

Mr Gujral: What else did you see there?

Seema: We went to the ancient temple of Kanya Kumari and walked up to the lighthouse. There were also the Gandhi Smarak and the famous Vivekananda Rock to see.

Mr Gujral: No shopping?

Seema: Oh, yes—lots of it. We spent hours looking at the exquisite shell handicrafts and colourful mats made of woven palm leaves. We also went boating and spent long hours on the beach and in the water, of course.

Mr Gujral: Your father and brother would have loved that, wouldn't they?

Seema: Oh, yes! We had to drag Nitin from the sea and Papa just would not stir from the quiet corners he found among rocks to relax with a book. You wouldn't know them both now because of their deep tan!

Mr Gujral: Well, Seema, I'm glad you enjoyed yourselves. And thanks for the unusual conch. I'll add it to my collection of shells.

Seema: That's wonderful—just what I thought.

Unit 5 Listening B

You come out of the Defence Officers' Colony and drive straight down Gulmohar Avenue, past the intersection with Rani Kunj Road. At the corner of Vaibhav Restaurant, you turn right on to Nehru Marg. You cut across P. C. Road and drive on, passing the bus depot on your right and the railway station on your left. At the intersection, you turn right on to Kamala Nagar Road and then take the first turning left to enter Mehta Lane. You drive to the end of the lane and find yourself facing the .... building across the street.

Unit 6 Listening

My dear young friends,

I am glad to see you before me, a flourishing band of young people who have chosen applied science as a profession.

I could sing hymns of praise with the refrain of the splendid progress in applied science that we have already made, and the enormous further progress that you will bring about. We are indeed in the era and in the native land of applied science. But it lies far from my thoughts to speak in this way. Why does this magnificent applied science, which saves work and makes life easier, bring us so little happiness? The simple answer runs: because we have not yet learned to make a sensible use of it.

In war it serves that we may poison and mutilate each other. In peace it has made our lives hurried and uncertain. Instead of freeing us in great measure from spiritually exhausting labour, it has made people into slaves of machinery, who for the most part complete their monotonous long day's work with disgust and must continually tremble for their poor rations.

You will be thinking that the old man sings an ugly song. I do it, however, with a good purpose, in order to point out a consequence.

It is not enough that you should understand about applied science in order that your work increases humanity's blessings.

Concern for human beings themselves and their fate must always form the chief interest of all technical endeavours; concern for the great involved problems of the organisation of labour and the distribution of goods, in order that the creation of our mind shall be a blessing and not a curse to humankind. Never forget this in the midst of your diagrams and equations.

From *Sigma XI quarterly*, 1938.

[Source: Sudarshanam's, *Technical English*, (Stirling Publishers, Delhi).]

Unit 7 Listening

Typical of the farmers who supply the Verka milk plant is Narain Singh, Verka village, Gurdaspur district. He settled here in 1967 with four acres of land. To supplement his farm income, he bought four buffaloes. But to deliver the milk he had to cycle 32 kms every day between his house and Batala, the nearest market. 'Milk is a perishable commodity; come rain or winter you have to deliver it,' said Narain Singh. 'In winter, there was no alternative than to brave the cold winds.'

'I immediately started supplying milk to the milk collection centre, when it was opened here at Mehta.' Mehta, one of the milk chilling centres attached to the Verka plant, in May 1992, eased his difficulties somewhat, as it was 10 kms from his house.

Real relief came to him in 1993 when a milk collection centre opened right in his village. 'Now I have to walk only a few paces to deliver the milk,' he added.

'Has it made any difference to you in terms of money,' I asked. 'Ah, yes. Now I am assured of a reasonable price,' replied Narain Singh. Also I can make the cash payment within ten days. In the olden days, we were at the mercy of the traders.

'Don't you find crop-raising more profitable than dairy farming?' I asked. 'No, this is more profitable. Only if my kids were slightly older, I would have gone in for 15 buffaloes instead of the eight I have now. Of the four acres of land, I devote two to cereals and the other two to fodder. From the two crops of wheat and rice every year, I shall sell about ten thousand rupees worth. The buffaloes give me at least 50,000 rupees a year in cash, apart from the milk, curd, lassi, butter and ghee we need.'

[Adapted from *Span*, 1997]

Unit 8 Listening

We know that the wild type organism is not mutated, i.e. its DNA, the base sequence in DNA has not undergone any change. But due to exposure to some physical or chemical mutagens some of the sequences of nucleotides may be changed and the wild type organism may undergo mutation to give a mutant type. So we can define mutation as any change in the base sequence of DNA and the agents which bring about mutation are referred to as mutagens. Mutagens are of three types: physical mutagens, chemical mutagens and biological mutagens. Mutagenesis is the process of producing mutation. Now let us discuss the types of mutation. In general, mutation may be of two types, spontaneous mutation and induced mutation. Spontaneous mutation occurs due to exposure to natural mutagens that is, spontaneous change in the nucleotide sequence of the DNA which later causes changes in the gene. That is the nature of the genetic material. Induced mutation is artificial mutation that is occurring due to exposure to specific mutagens. Another type of classification of mutation is point mutation and multiple mutation, which is based on the number of bases, which has undergone mutation. This can be further of different types: substitution mutation, insertion or addition mutation and deletion mutation.

Another type of mutation is based on the amino acid changes caused during the changes occurring in the nucleotide sequence. They are of different types: missense mutation, nonsense mutation and silent mutation. If a sense codon is changed to nonsense codon thereby terminating protein biosynthesis, it is referred to as nonsense mutation. Silent mutation occurs when even after mutation the same amino acid remains in the protein chain but there is a change in the nucleotide sequence. This is caused because of the degeneracy of the genetic code. Another classification of mutation is somatic mutation and germinal mutation which is dependent on the site of mutation, whether it takes place in the somatic cells or in the germ cells. There is another classification known as dominant mutation and recessive mutation. In dominant mutation, mutation produces a dominant gene, whereas in recessive mutation, it produces a recessive gene. Yet another type of mutation is back mutation or reverse mutation and forward mutation. Forward mutation occurs when a wild type is converted to a mutant type. When the mutant type is once again reverted back to the wild type because of second mutation, that is known as reverse mutation. Another type of mutation is macro mutation and micro mutation which is dependent on the size of the mutation occurring in the genotype. One more type of mutation is transition mutation and transversion mutation. In transition mutation a purine base or pyrimidine base may be converted to another purine base or pyrimidine base, whereas in a transversion mutation a purine base is converted into pyrimidine and pyrimidine base is converted into a purine base.

Now let us discuss the nature of the mutagens. Examples of physical mutagens are temperature, radiation—like x-rays, gamma rays (γ), αrays (alpha), β rays (beta), UV rays and infra red rays. The chemical mutagens are mustard gas, nitrous acid, nitrogen mustard, colchicine, formaldehyde, peroxides, caffeine and phenol. Examples of biological mutagens

are mutatorphages, transposons and certain retroviruses. Now the experimental proof for mutation was first studied by Muller in the year 1927, when he gave concrete experiments and interpretations regarding the occurrence of mutation and he did the experiments with drosophila and there are different reasons and molecular basis for mutagenesis that is a removal of an incorrectly inserted base which is prevented.

A base inserted that undergoes stortamarisation and a previously inserted base is chemically altered to the base having a different base pairing specificity—one or more bases skipped during replication and one or more extra bases inserted during replication. We can discuss in detail the mode of action of the different mutagens. The chemical mutagens can be classified into various types: base analogues, chemical mutagens, intercalating agents, mutator genes etc. A base analogue substitutes for a standard base during replication and causes a new base pair to appear in daughter cells in a later generation. Chemical mutagens such as nitrous acid, hydroxylamine, ethyl methatne suplhamate, MNG etc. (they) chemically alter a base so that a new base pair appears in daughter cells in a later generation. Intercalating agents, such as proflavins, which add or delete one or more base pairs by getting intercalated inside the DNA sequences. Some mutator genes cause some excessive insertion of incorrect bases or lack of repair of incorrectly inserted bases. Mutator genes will bring about mutation in other genes. So they are also considered mutagens. Now, what is meant by mutation rate? A number of mutations per gamete, per generation is referred to as mutation rate. In asexual organisms such as bacteria it is the number of mutations occurring per cell generation. What is meant by mutation frequency? It is the number of mutations in a population. It is high in e. coli than in human beings if we count the mutants over a period of time, say one year. So having learnt so much about mutation we should know what the effect of mutation is. Any mutation occurring in the genetic material that is DNA may alter the amino acid sequences in the protein that is the gene product and thereby it may even alter the nature of the genetic information and cause drastic changes in the inherited characters of human beings or any living organism.

Unit 9 Listening

Gary: Hello! At the Science Desk today, we find a report of a new way of treating seeds so that they can be planted at low temperatures. We'll hear the report at the end of the programme, but before we do that I've got a number of questions for our studio guest, our science reporter, Rita Black. Rita...thank you for joining us once again at the Science Desk.

Rita: It's a pleasure as always, Gary.

Gary: This new treatment for seeds has been developed by a commercial organisation in the United States. And my first question is, why, why have they done it?

Rita: Well, my first answer, Gary, is simple, money. So how can it work? The use of genetic engineering in seeds has made huge advances in some areas in terms of increasing crop yields or perhaps making better crops. Bigger, riper tomatoes, for example. Uhm, these seeds cost a lot of money because of all the research work which has had to go into them. And it is still a risk when you plant them, because if you plant them too early—we are really talking here about countries which have real seasons and real temperature differences between the seasons—if you plant them too early, the ground can be too cold or too wet, and this can increase the possibility of attack from fungi. Now you could use genetic engineering to fight those fungi as well, but that's a little bit more difficult than increasing crop yields. If you plant the seeds too late, that means effectively your growing season is shorter, so you won't grow as much crops. So that's why companies are looking for this kind of solution.

Gary: Well, you've explained the problem that farmers face around the world. Be more precise about the solution that these American scientists have provided.

Rita: Okay, well, it's quite an intuitive solution, I think in that you might protect something from the rain by wrapping it up. That's what they are suggesting you should do with these seeds. You just wrap it in some plastic and then you can put it in the ground and it sits there. The water in the ground can't get to it, and neither can the fungi. Now they are using a particular kind of wrapping called shrink-wrapping which is where you put some plastic over the thing that you want to wrap up, and then in some way, perhaps by applying heat, you cause the plastic to shrink, so the whole thing is kind of nicely contained. That's what they are doing with these seeds.

Gary: Well, let's hear part of today's report. And we'll start with the beginning of the report. And that comes from you, Rita.

Rita: Well, the seeds produced commercially today are the results of very good genetic engineering programmes. So, the seeds themselves have great potential. However farmers in seasonal climates have to take a big risk in deciding when they actually put the seeds into the ground. Plant them too late and they will have a short growing season and yields will suffer. Plant them earlier and the seeds have the possibility of producing more crop, but they will also be in cold wet soil, which can lead to fungal attack and other diseases. Now a group of chemists in a biotechnology company in the USA think they can eliminate this dilemma altogether by shrink-wrapping seeds in a new type of plastic.

Gary: So, that's the basic concept, Rita, and we will move straight on to the American scientist who has invented the new technique. And that's Dr Mary Stewart. She is speaking on the telephone here and begins by explaining what she and her colleagues have been doing.

Dr Stewart: What we've been doing is developing a polymer which can prevent moisture from going into seeds if conditions in the soil are detrimental to the seed at that time. These are basically plastics we make from modified vegetable oils.

Gary: Once the seed has been shrink-wrapped, what happens? How does this coating work? How does it help?

Rita: First of all, you put the seeds in the ground and if the ground is cold and wet then the coating will remain intact, will remain impermeable to moisture. Moisture can't get through and obviously fungi and other agents that can damage it can't get through, either. The crucial point here is at some point this shrink-wrapping has to come off; otherwise the seed will never develop. So, they have been quite clever here. What they've done is they've said, 'Let's look for the temperature where we would like a seed to start developing and let's make the shrink-wrapping fall apart at precisely that temperature. So, let's say you've put the seeds in the ground, it's cold, the seed warms up as the earth itself warms up and eventually the

shrink-wrapping becomes permeable—water can seep through—and eventually the coating falls apart and the seed can grow.'

Gary: Well, let's hear what Dr Stewart has to say about the financial viability of using the new seeds.

Dr Stewart: We believe that the farmer will make significantly more money by using these seeds. Currently losses from seeds that die in the ground are very extensive. So small increases in the amounts of germination in the number of seeds will readily pay for the value of the coating cost.

Gary: A small increase in the amount of germination in the number of seeds that grow will pay for the coating, says Dr Mary Stewart. Thank you once again for joining us today, Rita. We've been discussing a report about shrink-wrapped seeds.

[Adapted from *BBC Science Desk*]

Instructions to the users of the CD accompanying this book

The CD accompanying the book is both an audio CD, which can be played on an audio CD player, and also a computer CD, containing a program that can run on a personal computer.

To use in a computer, just place the CD in the tray. If 'autoplay' is active on your computer, the program will start on its own. If 'autoplay' is not active you will have to browse through the CD and click on the file 'Learning English.exe'.

Once the program, begins you will be offered the choice of

1. Listening to the audio CD
2. Running the computer program

To run the computer program, select the second option and click OK. You will be presented with the text of Unit 1 Listening Exercise A.

To select any other unit, click on the 'down-arrow' on the title and select the unit from the dropped-down list.

To select an exercise, click the 'down-arrow' on the second line and choose the exercise from the list.

To listen to the audio, click on the 'Play' button on the task bar at the top right.

To pause while playing, click on the same button (which will now be labelled 'Pause').

To stop (so as to restart from the beginning), click on the 'Stop' button. (It will be available only if you are playing).

To move to another exercise in the unit being viewed or to another unit, click on the 'Stop' button, and then either click on the 'down-arrow' on the second line, and select the desired exercise or do the same on the 'down-arrow' on the title and choose the required unit.

The line in the text that is being read out will be highlighted (in red) in the text.

To play starting from a particular line, click (when you have stopped playing) on the line. It will become highlighted. Now click the 'Play' button. The text will be read out from there onwards. If you wish to play only that line, keep the 'Ctrl' key pressed while you click on the 'Play' button.

For help at any stage, click on the 'Help' button on the task-bar (top right).

To adjust the volume, drag the volume marker up (to increase) or down (to decrease).

To quit the program, click the 'Quit' button at the right extreme of the task bar.

You can move between pages of text by clicking the buttons labelled: '<', '>', '<<', '>>'. Try it and see.

If you choose the 'audio CD' option (when you run the program on the computer), then Windows media player will start and the CD will begin to play from Track 1. You will also be presented with a track list giving the track number of the required exercise. To jump to any other track, double click on the track in the play list pane on the right (not on the track list). (If the play list is not visible, go to the menu 'View >> Now Playing Options' and click 'Show Play list')

To use the CD on an audio CD player, just place the CD in the tray and press 'Play'. Use the track list given below to select the track of the desired exercise.

System requirements

To play the CD, you will need a PC with a CD drive, a sound card and speakers. If it to be used as a presentation in a classroom, a large format monitor or video card with a TV out facility and a TV would be required. The PC should have Windows 98, Windows ME or Windows XP as the operating system.

Windows media player should be installed on the system.

The installable versions of Windows media player (freeware from Microsoft) are provided in the 'misc' folder on the CD. If you need to instal the player, then do as follows.

If your OS is Windows XP, run MPSetupXP.exe.

If your OS is Windows ME or Windows 98 (SE), then run MPSetup.exe.

If your OS is Windows 98 (First Edition), then run MP71.exe.

The track numbers on the audio CD of the various exercises are:

		Track
Unit 1		
	Listening Exercise A	1
	Listening Exercise B	2
	Speaking (Dialogue 1: Formal)	3
	Speaking (Dialogue 2: Informal)	4
	Speaking Exercise A	5
	Speaking Exercise B	6
Unit 2		
	Listening Exercise	7
	Speaking (Dialogue 1: Formal)	8
	Speaking Exercise A	9
	Speaking (Dialogue 2: Formal)	10
	Speaking (Dialogue 3: Informal)	11
	Speaking Exercise B	12
Unit 3		
	Listening Exercise A	13
	Listening Exercise B	14
	Speaking (Dialogue 1: Formal)	15
	Speaking (Dialogue 2: Informal)	16
	Speaking (Dialogue 3: Formal)	17
	Speaking Exercise A	18
Unit 4		
	Listening Exercise	19
	Speaking (Dialogue 1: Formal)	20
	Speaking (Dialogue 2: Informal)	21
	Speaking Exercise A	22
Unit 5		
	Listening Exercise A	23
	Listening Exercise B	24
	Speaking (Dialogue 1: Formal)	25
	Speaking (Dialogue 2: Informal)	26
	Speaking Exercise A	27
Unit 6		
	Listening	28
	Speaking (Dialogue 1: Formal)	29
	Speaking (Dialogue 2: Formal)	30
	Speaking (Dialogue 3: Informal)	31
	Speaking Exercise A	32
Unit 7		
	Listening	33
	Speaking (Dialogue 1)	34
	Speaking (Dialogue 2)	35
	Speaking (Dialogue 3)	36
	Speaking Exercise A	37
Unit 8		
	Speaking (Dialogue 1)	38
	Speaking (Dialogue 2)	39
	Speaking (Dialogue 3)	40
	Speaking Exercise A	41
Unit 9		
	Listening	42
	Speaking (Dialogue 1)	43
	Speaking (Dialogue 2)	44
	Speaking Exercise A	45